THE FIRE AND THE BONFIRE

A JOURNEY INTO MEMORY

ARDYN HALTER

ISBN 9789493276857 (ebook)

ISBN 9789493276833 (paperback)

ISBN 9789493276840 (hardcover)

Publisher: Amsterdam Publishers, The Netherlands

info@amsterdampublishers.com

The Fire and the Bonfire is part of the series Holocaust Heritage

Copyright © Ardyn Halter, 2023

Cover design by Ardyn Halter

All Rights Reserved. No part of this publication may be reproduced or transmitted in any form or by any means, electronic or mechanical, including photocopy, recording or any other information storage and retrieval system, without prior permission in writing from the publisher.

CONTENTS

1. An early painting — 1
2. Trusting early memories — 4
3. Placing a stone — 8
4. Closure — 14
5. A Book — 17
6. Retracing — 23
7. Ghetto heritage — 26
8. Oil and glass — 28
9. Frozen frames or continuity — 32
10. Rwanda – why Rwanda? — 34
11. Who cares? — 38
12. Crossing a line — 40
13. Aloma's challenge — 43
14. Incomplete — 45
15. Snapshots — 47
16. Grandparents on paper — 49
17. Inner screens — 51
18. Anomalous — 53
19. Involving the next generation — 56
20. Avalanche — 58
21. Shoah – some definitions — 60
22. Time to tell — 61
23. Rwanda notes 1: Circling — 64
24. Patriarchal — 68
25. Necessary space — 70
26. Rwanda notes 2: Fungi — 72
27. Tidal — 76
28. Rwanda notes 3: Black — 79
29. Driving to Chodecz — 82
30. Adjustments — 85
31. Two peoples — 88
32. Rwanda notes 4: The windows — 91
33. Blue — 95
34. Can you ever go back? — 97
35. Chodecz — 101

36. Recognition and Rozia	104
37. The mound	106
38. Rwanda notes 5: Tell the world	109
39. Somewhere my Father was meant to go	113
40. The first death camp	117
41. Read this or move on a few pages	121
42. A container	128
43. An after-dinner dinner with family Mojta	133
44. Lens reality	139
45. Reality and friendship	141
46. Two lakes	143
47. Duck shoot	146
48. Numbers in water	149
49. A hunting lodge in Lodz	154
50. The barber's hands	156
51. Lapidary	162
52. Pools	165
53. Medals	169
54. Going to the movies	174
55. Measure for measure	176
56. Fatigue & fremd	178
57. A walk in Auschwitz-Birkenau	180
58. Other visitors	185
59. Street scene	188
60. Carrying on	190
61. Dresden	192
62. The escape from the forest – Version 1	197
63. A meeting with Avraham Sztajer	202
64. The same eyes	205
65. The escape – The second version	208
66. The promise	214
67. The kindness of strangers	217
68. Moving ashes	219
69. How much is too much?	221
70. Book without shelf	225
71. A visit to Karmiel	227
72. A simple bonfire	233

Notes	235
Acknowledgments	237
About the Author	239
Amsterdam Publishers Holocaust Library	241

To my parents: Susie and Roman Halter
who found the strength to live after the Shoah
and shared their love and appetite for life.

Besides direct testimony there is a substantial, growing body of writing by the Second Generation, those born to survivors.

I am offering this book as a different perspective, whilst conscious nonetheless that I am, in actual fact, merely adding yet another pebble to the pile.

*This book was commenced in 2005
and completed in 2014.
My father, Roman Halter died in 2012.
My mother, Susie Halter, née Nador, died in 2015.*

Bonfire: [BONEsb. 1+ FIRE = fire of bones. The etymological spelling bone-fire, Sc. Bane-fire, was common down to 1760, though bonfire was also in use from the 16thc., and became more common as the original sense was forgotten. Johnson in 1755 decided for bonfire, "from bon good, (Fr) and fire". But the shortening of the vowel was natural, from its position; cf. knowledge, Monday, collier, etc. In Scotland with the form bane-fire, the memory of the original sense was retained longer; for the annual midsummer "banefire" or "bonfire" in the burgh of Hawick, old bones were regularly collected and stored up, down to c. 1800]

† 1. A fire of bones; a great fire in which bones were burnt in the open air. Obs. (The 17th century quotations are chiefly allusive, implying a knowledge that bone-fires ought to burn bones.)....
† 2. A fire in which to consume corpses, a funeral pile, a pyre. THE OED
p. 985

1

AN EARLY PAINTING

Roman Halter, The Seven Men, painting

"Who are those men?" I asked my father.

"We escaped into the forest," he replied. "It was night. I was the last to go and I ran in a zig-zag so if they shot at me I would have a chance. The bullets might miss me. I made it to the trees. For a long time I could not find them in the darkness. Then I saw them."

I remember the silence after those words. So perhaps he did not say anything more.

Then I counted the heads. Six. "Is that a seventh man at the back there?" I asked.

That is all I remember of those words. If he did say anything more, I cannot remember it. I did not think of asking him why he had painted those men or what happened to them.

It was almost forty years before I realised that there were two versions in his mind. One that he wrote to protect himself, the other what really had happened. For all those years those haunting faces had hammered at his memory. They returned to haunt him. He could not sleep easy because he believed that he had been unable to save them. They were there in his mind, six or seven faces without eyes, facing him. No. One of the faces he painted had an eye, Cyclops-open, staring directly at him from the centre of the painting. The rest were shadowed. Shaven heads, tough features, confronting him, as accusingly as the judges in Georges Rouault's paintings confront the viewer, that was the way I responded to my father's painting the first time I saw those men, when I was nine.

Who were they? What happened to them?

Go back to what is clear in memory; me watching him paint. I am seven years old. I know this because his painting is dated 1963. By then we had moved to Albert Mansions, a solid residential block of flats at the top of Crouch Hill with a panoramic view south over all of London, clear to St Paul's cathedral and beyond to the North Downs. My father worked on a tall white metal stool with a thick pine seat at his architect draftsman's table and I sat on a tarpaulin on the close-grained Douglas fir-panelled floor with my colours and paper. He soaked thick watercolour paper in cold water and held it over the sink while the water ran off to one corner. Then he placed it flat on a sheet of hardboard, sponged off the surface and smoothed it. He gum-taped the edges to a board and left it to dry propped against the pine-panelled wall.

When the paper had dried and stretched, he built up washes of progressively darker pigments – Naples yellow, yellow-ochre, raw Sienna, Alizarin red, burnt umber, and sepia and, finally, black. He worked in layer over layer and then wetted them and blotted back, revealing the lighter colours beneath. The faces emerged from deep darkness. The stark, shaven heads all seemed the same at first. Yet they were different. It became apparent that my father was remembering particular people, looming out of darkness. They looked like obscure, severe versions of the faces in his book of Byzantine mosaics. But whereas those were archetypal, impersonal and solemn, these faces my father painted were sombre and frightening, somehow *known* individuals.

He worked and reworked the painting, darkening it further in more washes and blotting back the noses and cheeks and foreheads to reveal the lighter tones beneath. The eye sockets were dark. They could see him, but he could not see them.

Then, when he glazed the painting in a glossy watercolour varnish, it was finished and he could not change it any more. The faces were set in the darkness. They were fixed and would neither advance further into light or detail, nor would they retreat back into pure sepia.

The painting was framed but then never hung. I don't know where he put it. After he died, I found it in the loft. Through direct contact, the glass of the frame had stuck to the varnish and it was difficult to separate them without tearing the paper.

By then or, to be precise, two years after his death, I knew what had happened to those men, to two of them, specifically, and the fate of the others.

2

TRUSTING EARLY MEMORIES

Travelling with my mother and sister on the upper deck of the old, glossy, grenadier-red London buses into the West End, to Lyons Corner House and the Start-Rite shoe shop on Oxford Street, we passed a horse-drawn milk cart turning from Crouch Hill and Mount View Road. The bus journey in my memory is, in fact, an amalgam of three routes, the old 212, the 259 and the 14, all double-deckers. I know this because the places remembered do not belong to one route. Memory has conflated them into a journey seen from the upper deck with the following frames: the occasional car drives by, names long gone – Hillman, Humber, Singer, Sunbeam, Commer; a brewer's cart delivers barrels of beer to The Stapleton pub; the team of Percherons stand, stamping the street, their heads in feed sacks, coughing oats, hot breath steaming; a mile closer to town, the steel tramlines gleam between cobbles, snaking their double twin tracks from Finsbury Park to Gower Street. And in the thick, late autumn afternoon, a coal-smog fog is waiting somewhere to swallow the daylight whole.

Along the route, even then, fifteen years after the end of the war, there are still bombsites from the Blitz. They are piled with rubble, the adjacent buildings and terraces buttressed with massive wooden beams. The exposed cross-sections of houses show patterned wallpaper changing from landing to landing, some of them revealing other patterned papers beneath, under-skins, previous lives, torn lengths of colours. These were not cross-sections of giant dolls houses. They were the homes of real people. Aged four, this may have been a first consciousness of the past as something amounting to more than what I had been given to eat or what we had done yesterday. The past meant other lives and places, homes that once were and now existed no more. The word "war" did not yet mean anything to me but, frequently, it entered into adult conversations – "before the war", "during the war", "since the war".

Round about the same time, the West End of London was peppered with beggars, crippled ex-servicemen who might have been incapacitated in either the First or the Second World War – there was no difference to me. These remainders, these reduced people, had pitches on Piccadilly and Oxford Street. To my child's eye they belonged to the stretch of road in the same way as the shoeshine men with their large wooden boxes and brass foot-stands, and tins of rich smelling Kiwi wax, pavement figures who polished shoes to army parade standard, or the sandwich men walking up and down the pavement like the playing-card gardeners in my sister's book *Alice in Wonderland*.

Every English man and woman had known war as an adult or a child, on the home or battle front. London still had a residual military air. It was regimented – queues for buses, not a foot out of line, a dress code ... spit only with polish. There was still conscription – it ended in 1962.

Some of the beggars had one leg, an empty trouser tucked up behind and pinned with a safety pin. Others had no legs and sat on cushions, on the pavement, their dwarf crutches neatly placed, flat, one on top of another. These stocky little men sat at my boy-head height with signs beside them and medals on their chest or on a threadbare velvet remnant close to an upturned hat containing a few coppers. I was mesmerized and not a little afraid of one beggar, a veteran, who had no legs and only one arm with which he played a harmonica. Did my mother say to me "Once he had legs and two arms", or did I think that? I became hazily conscious of times that preceded the present. A city before my arrival just as it began to dawn on me that there must have been a world before everyone's arrival – buildings preceding bombsites, other buildings before them and, possibly, trees or fields before them. And it was logical that there must be the same back sequence for people too. Crippled men with legs, men who had been boys and babies. A mother must once have mothered that limbless harmonica player. What would she have thought had she seen her boy at his pitch on Piccadilly, limbless, playing ... what? I have no recollection of the tune.

Everything went back, everyone had once been younger, different, including my own parents. Every journey implied a reverse journey, a time when Aloma, my sister, was around before me and when my parents were there, before her, just them.

And that photo of my parents, standing in swim suits, tanned, on a rock in the sea – near Capri – the image of sporting health. At some point I sought to square this with a gradual awareness of their carrying within them an earlier world, life before my arrival, before that sun-soaked image, stories of privation, starvation, death, murder, war and, on my father's side, of a family he had once had, and on my mother's side of parents she had but could not see because they were on the other side of an Iron Curtain? I consigned my mother's parents and my father's, together, to the world of once. Once. To a child the past is summed up in that word. Once – distant as a horizon, as distant as "upon a time".

My parents' tanned bodies – my father deeply bronzed, my mother more burnt than brown – matched a proud physical reality, which is to say that they both exuded a pride in the physical – and as a child I was proud of that pride. In memory I connect it to the distinctive nutty (walnut) smell of Ambre Solaire. This physical world stood against a dreadful past, no, not even against it, or versus – for the past was not physically present but it was more like squares, vacant plots of absence, that over years formed an immaterial, intangible patchwork. And yet, with passing time, it was increasingly palpable, like an invisible object, one that is only seen and felt by the shadows it casts.

3

PLACING A STONE

Placing a pebble on a Jewish grave is an act of memory. Walk through a Jewish cemetery, and, by the stones, you can see whose grave has been recently visited, who has been thought of, who has had a *yahrzeit*. By inference you can also tell whose memory has been neglected, or which graves are not visited.

There are two stones on this one, higgledy-piggledy rows of stones on that one there. You might assume a multiplicity of visitors when in actual fact, perhaps, each stone over there, on that grave, was left by the same person, week after week, carefully, thoughtfully, or just habitually. Beyond this, I am not sure what the numbers of stones have to tell about the dead or those still living. Yet, on visits to cemeteries, it is hard also to avoid these comparisons, they lie buried so close, so close together.

Pebbles last longer than flowers that, as they wilt, after a day or so, seem to emphasise neglect. The pebbles are memorial markers. They are thoughts, prayers, presences.

Each of the thousands of books written about the Shoah, the genocide of Europe's Jews is, like a pebble, an act of commemoration. No single one can suffice, nor will they ever, collectively, serve as adequate memorials to genocide.

Adequate.

Feelings of inadequacy numb the mind of visitors departing the sites of mass-murder, death camps, locations of execution. No film or book is "adequate". There is always an inevitable sense of incompleteness.

So why add yet another pebble to the pile?

There are tens of thousands of testimonies of survivors, set down for their families (living and dead) published (like my own father's) or unpublished, filmed or recorded, for their families, for posterity, stored in Yad Vashem, Yale, or the Holocaust Memorial Archive based in the University of Southern California. The latter contains 52,000 filmed testimonies that exist because Steven Spielberg ploughed all the profits from *Schindler's List* into a vast recording project and because survivors, at some point during the years of ordeal, swore to themselves and to their murdered kin that the world would know what was done. In most cases because many also shared the hope that the world, knowing, would learn, learn and prevent another genocide from recurring.

For many, the recording of their testimonies meant breaking the silence of decades, peeling back thin skin covering deep, unhealed wounds. They sought, in their telling, to name the dead, family and friends and draw them back from the oblivion their murderers intended for them.

At the end of the Second World War my father made a journey back to Chodecz, his home-town in Poland, in the hope of finding other members of his family alive. War divided up his family and destroyed them. His father starved to death in the Lodz Ghetto. His mother and sister and two of his cousins were exterminated in Chelmno, other siblings were killed in Auschwitz, Treblinka, in Russia and the Warsaw Ghetto. My father escaped as his transport set out from the Lodz ghetto for the Chelmno extermination camp. He survived the selection at Auschwitz and then was transported in winter, in a cattle truck (as part of a group of slave-labourers) to Stutthof by the Baltic where only a third survived the first two months. The group was then moved to Dresden where they worked in forced labour in a munitions factory before and during the Allied bombings and fire storms before being taken on a death march from which he escaped and, somehow, was taken in by a German couple in the countryside outside Dresden. At the end of the war he returned to Chodecz, endangering his life – locals assumed the thin teenager was returning to reclaim his family's property and sought to kill him. Realising that none of his family would return, my father made his way to Theresienstadt where child and youth survivors were gathered. Together with them he was transported to England.

In 2005, like countless other survivors who returned with their families, in the 1980s, 1990s and later, to their hometowns and places of murder, he, my sister Aloma and I intended to retrace that journey. He had been back before, once in 1967 and had made other visits since then, though not to his hometown. Although this was a journey we had spoken about making for almost a decade, shortly before we left father had arranged for an independent film crew to accompany us. This meant it would not be possible to simply "be" with our father – inevitably, my sister and I would be a supporting cast. The proximity of a lens would replace and preclude real intimacy. The quietly humane yet forceful voice of my father's public persona would be speaking, inevitably, beyond us to a television audience and to posterity. And he preferred that. There would be no words that might include doubt, uncertainty, puzzlement, questions, even a seeking – together with us – to clarify points, facts, places, or even discover things. It seemed as if he wanted our relations to be seen from the outside.

The film, like so many films and books, would follow a trail of perpetuated memory, setting down the survivor's story. And for my father the core facts mattered most of all – to give the lie to deniers of the Shoah. I felt uncomfortable because his story was known to me. And it was familiar to Aloma. She was in the process of editing his book, or rather finally editing it, since over several years he had sent her and me countless pages of manuscript to read and comment on, edit and return. It was wearing and felt interminable. And this had to stop. Aloma had been a professional editor for many years and she had decided to take on the project, complete it, end it. The final version had to be brought out. Aloma had found a publisher.

So to pretend to hear those memories for the first time was absurd. In reality we would be comparing what he said with his previous accounts, verbal and written.

For father the formal presence of a film crew was possibly strategic, a way for him to avoid revealing memories he did not wish to touch upon. In teaming with the interests of the film he could thus avoid uncomfortable moments from his past. Neither Aloma nor I wished to act the part of first-time listeners. The linear assumptions of the film enterprise made no allowance for the inconsistencies of memory – the different words chosen to describe the same event and the changing refraction of light on those experiences with the passing of time. Would it not be possible, even more interesting, more true, at this point in time, to examine and record how what we would see matched our expectations? His with his own memories, ours against what we had heard and read, for so long?

There were really three very different things going on, three agendas of questionable compatibility: the film; my father's journey; and my sister's and my own perceptions. A film would demand to follow a pattern of revelation in an ambience of filial piety. I found myself thinking that there must be a different approach, a truer way to film such a journey, one that would not place my sister and me in the role of funnels, passive receptors.

It might be interesting to compare the way a survivor sees things twenty and then 60 years on, or examine how he has transmitted his experiences to the next generation, decade by decade, and do so by recording our perceptions of what we had heard. If one is to talk about "continuity" then surely an analysis of this was crucial to it – an understanding of changing memory, the historicity not only of the way perception of history changes within a society, over decades, but also within the life-span of an individual.

The on-going transference of knowledge is itself a mode of experience – one which my sister and I had lived with for so long. Would it count for nothing?

That journey in 2005 was one, but not the only, catalyst for this book, for, periodically, over three decades, I have made other journeys of the mind. Call them journeys or efforts, commemorative and creative, paintings, stained-glass windows, attempts, essays – in the Montaignesque sense of that word, *essais*.

Montaigne wore a medallion around his neck engraved with the words *"Que sais-je?"* Everything he experienced (with the notable exception of religious beliefs) was subject to empirical scrutiny. Nothing was taken for granted. All of my *essais* to approach the subject of the Shoah have failed, in some significant measure, because the Shoah is unapproachable, disorientating in its scale.

A submarine navigating obscure depths, transmitting sonar, informs as much about its own position, the source of the sonar, as it does about any sounded object. That journey with my sister and my father to Poland and Germany was in itself an *essai*. I offer this book and my personal reflections in the hope that they may help others to realise what Sir Christopher Ricks has called "the shortcomings of the sympathetic imagination."[1]

Ardyn Halter, The Family I Never Knew - oil on canvas 200 x 208 cm, 1981

4

CLOSURE

To make a journey – unlike a holiday – one must be prepared to step outside oneself, beyond mental comfort or familiarity. Most journeys move forwards, promising the unknown. A true journey takes one to a different inner place, and by journey's end you are not the same as you were when you set out.

Our journey back to Poland also had an unforeseen result, different to the downward, backward motion, my father, sister, the film crew and I were mentally keyed for. The archetype for such journeys is Odysseus's descent into Hades to visit the souls of the dead. Such descents are patterned in literature through Virgil and Dante, or in reduced form, simply stencilled in all the "roots" projects undertaken by children at school or when people leaf back through old family albums and then say "Let's go back there to see the old places, see where we came from." Go back. But all journeys back actually take place in the present. They are less concerned with the past than with how images and experiences are maintained in memory and released into the present.

Gabriel Garcia Marquez has said that life is not what you were but what you can recall and how you remember that, in order to tell it. As the decades pass, life seems to me less and less tangible, the unknown vaster than ever. In the impalpable mist of the unknown, images stored, hoarded in memory, sometimes seem the most tangible things I know. They are like building blocks.

Particular memories may feel as though they are more solid than the present. It's strange but true. Memories can seem more solid, though less immediate than, for example, a person sitting before me when I am drawing her or him. For a sitter can seem as protean as daylight in the studio, or as a mood or the touch of graphite on paper. Giacometti once said: "What is a head? What is a nose? I do not know. And with time I know even less." Yet – and this is crucial to the experience I am seeking to set down in this book – even memories, images that do not move in light, do not stay still. The telling of those moments alters them. Words reshape them, even when you feel most confident that you are cupping those very nuggets of existence.

The Chodecz we came to, my father's birthplace, was a town stripped of any sign that a Jew had ever lived or even died there. Not a *mezuzah* on a doorpost, no *Magen David* over a door, or in ironwork on a Jewish shop, not one Jewish tombstone. The purge was total. In a town that once had been half-Jewish. The graveyard had been bulldozed and covered with a mound of earth and planted with birch and elms. Every mark of the past Jewish presence was effaced. By the Nazis, or also after the Nazis? Nothing remained. Save what existed in my father's head or in his paintings or his writing. Nothing more.

There is the notion that spirits can be set to rest. But only time and oblivion does that, helped or hindered by us.

I cannot deny harbouring a weak, clichéd hope that the journey and then, perhaps this book, might bring closure to something with which I have lived since my childhood. Yet if that was what I really thought, then I was wrong, just as I know that writing this is unlikely to be my last thought on the subject.

So putting aside closure, or other metaphors implying completion, I understood that at best perhaps I might assemble pieces within a mental puzzle, pin images to places, dates, words, faces or signs. At the very least we would physically see places my father had mentioned or about which I had read. These had, like any story told to you as a child, established themselves through imagination as mental images, so perhaps one might more correctly call the sites we would visit "the places of those places".

The late mayor of Jerusalem, Teddy Kollek, used to say "We die twice. Once, when we physically die; twice, when we are forgotten." All good aphorisms lay claim to deference, the silent appreciation warranted by the wisdom of the fathers, biblical in weight. (That Kollek employed this particular one as a potent fundraiser for municipal projects validates rather than invalidates it.) I've often heard that dictum reverberate in a room or, later, in my mind: "Twice when we are forgotten." Hearing it, inescapably, images of broken gravestones come to mind, carved inscriptions, weatherworn, lichen-spotted, tilting into the sunken ground, their dates and names, legends and symbols unintelligible.

5

A BOOK

When I was nine years old I came across a book near my father's desk. Our library was small and I was allowed to browse the art books. But this was one of three books that were set aside. I was alone in the room. The book I opened was the largest of the three. I skipped a couple of pages of text and then, there in black and white, was the photo of a bulldozer shovelling piles of emaciated naked bodies. The title read *Bergen-Belsen 1945*.

It was the most brutal image I had ever seen. Revulsion rapidly overcame my curiosity. After looking for perhaps another half minute at this, and one or two other photographs, I felt as though I had been hit across my face, and I also felt guilty. I closed the book and replaced it beneath the other two books, spine towards me, and left the room.

This photo was part of my father's past. But what part? And why, if it was part of his past, did he need to have the book? If he had lived through such scenes why did he need reminding? Why did he wish to be reminded of this? Or had he lived through it but not seen them. Had they happened while he was there, but not before his eyes? What did these photos mean to him? Seeing such photos, was he learning things that he had heard of but did not know? And was seeing the only real knowledge? So many questions, many only half-formed, turning over in my mind. Questions I could not voice.

Some time round about then at my school, The Haberdashers' Aske's, the Headmaster announced on a Monday morning in assembly, that a boy from the school (I think his surname was Rose) had died. He had been very ill and had then died or he had drowned over the weekend – perhaps my memory is conflating two deaths that occurred at roughly the same time. By Monday afternoon I could not picture Rose. It was strange that a face I must have seen, passed in the playground, perhaps even spoken to, failed to appear in my memory. On the way home from school I asked a classmate to describe him to me but it was no use. He couldn't either. If anything our effort confused matters – Rose was lost. I tried to imagine Rose drowning and saw various faces, one on a pillow surrounded by parents and a grim-faced doctor, another of a head gulping water, but the image strayed off and became a swimmer, swimming front-crawl, opening his mouth to breathe on the hollow of his head-wave, and there were turquoise tiles somewhere to the side, with sunlight and the water's reflection playing patterns on them.

And I wondered if those books of photos were my father's way of preserving the memory of what he had gone through. Perhaps they were a reality he had experienced but not seen, like the drowning or death of Rose who had been with me yet I could no longer recall his face, as well as an independent reference, his way of knowing and understanding, in case he forgot.

For me, those photos were a form of coming-of-age. I began to think he left them there for us to discover. They confirmed our family's past as unspeakably dreadful.

Centre of Chodecz

Memory is different from commemoration because memory is personal. Commemoration is general.

For my father, the thought of his father's death in the Lodz Gehtto, of his father dead, was inextricably linked to the personal memory he had of burying his father, of lugging the stretcher himself, by himself, in the cemetery, turning it end over end, in his weakened and starved condition, towards a grave he had prepared, watched by his mother who was physically too weak to help him.

If none of the specific places where his family died, where their bones and ashes mingled with earth and water could be found, I wondered if it would be fitting to create a memorial to them all? And if so, where? Where they died or once lived? My father's book would be a truer memorial. A book as a place – more real than chiselled stone, telling of the diaspora of murder, truer than a chiselled gravestone that suggests a semblance of normalcy. For a gravestone is a marker, laying claim to presence in that place on this earth, to normalcy of existence.

If, for a survivor, a gravestone signifies completion, then what completion is it? Would it lay memory to rest and make things right? If it is a *mitzvah*, a good deed, then where exactly is the good? To whom? To my father, or to the memory of his father?

The commemorative stone of one who has died in his or her sleep – should it be the same as for one who was dispossessed, humiliated, dehumanized, starved, reduced? A decent burial is after all a human right, a basic human right. So should a grave for such a person record the fact that the deceased was murdered, brutally, inhumanly deprived of his or her rights?

On the occasions I have designed and made memorials to the victims of genocide I have always been hounded by a sense of the inadequacy of every such memorial. Obviously, memorials provide evidence, physical loci for commemorative gathering, facts on the ground to help educate future generations, facts that stand up to those people who deny the figures, reduce them, the historical revisionists. Yet sometimes I find myself thinking that only emptiness, vacancy could ever really communicate their loss and our (my) helplessness in communicating it.

There is a Shoah memorial in the German town of Saarbrücken where every cobblestone has been sandblasted by German artist Jochen Gerz with the name of a Jew from town who was deported, and the date of her or his deportation. But the cobblestones have been laid facedown. The inscription is not there to be seen. All that is there is a sign telling the visitor or the locals that this has been done, that the town's *Platz* and every square cobblestone in it bears the name of a Jewish person who once lived there and who is no more. The inscriptions cannot be worn down. They face the earth. The memorial communicates vacancy and loss as no other memorial I know or have heard of. It compels one to think and, at the same time, to acknowledge the inadequacy of such thought.

Going to visit a memorial site and creating a memorial are two very different things. The one is contemplative, the other only partly contemplative. The activity of working on a project at some point in the project supplants contemplation of the subject. The working process effectively often distance one from it. You are so close that you can hardly see or feel.

You have an idea, a concept. And then you must make it. There you are working at it, sketching, enlarging, cutting, measuring, selecting glass, making moulds, casting – all physical acts to focus on. Chisel, chisel. Vermillion or carmine? Sky blue or ultramarine? This activity supplants thought about the subject of the work. In fact the busier you are then the less you think about the subject. Once the idea is fixed, or the design is evolved, the key rationale completed, the decisions are largely aesthetic. Commemoratively speaking, you are devoting months of your life to that purpose, but of that time only a tithe – possibly less – is engaged in actively *thinking* about the subject. More than this would probably impair the work.

Over five years my father and I worked to create Yad LaYeled, a building in the north of Israel, the only educational centre in the world commemorating the one-and-a-half-million Jewish children who were murdered during the Shoah. We established a degree of common thought which resulted in the design. The building was to be like a simplified child's sand castle and would feature stained-glass windows interpreting the children's drawings from Theresienstadt – gathered after the Second World War in the book *No More Butterflies in the Ghetto*. The images made by children *then* should provide a link to children and adults visiting the memorial museum *now*.

For a decade, due to a variety of reasons, we had postponed the journey to Poland. Discussion of it would arise and then be left aside. Some reasons were medical – my father's triple bypass or his diabetes, others were connected to my work, painting, exhibitions, printmaking, commissions, other family commitments. We had settled that we would go together whilst we could. Aloma joined us because she felt that without coming she would not be able to complete her editing of Roman's book.

He had said that he would go with me alone and then return later in the year with her and our mother and sister Aviva. But Aloma said,

"Postpone me coming with you – postpone your book." A clear indication to him that there were points that needed clarifying in order to complete her editing. A degree of openness was required, an intimacy beyond that which, so far, he had recorded in all the draft chapters of his book. For her this was part of the promise of this journey.

My mother followed the preparations with some interest but possibly did not want to go to Chodecz, knowing that my father had returned there in 1967 with a lady who for some years had shared his architectural practice, who was, in effect, his second partner, with whom he lived off and on. Even more than this she may not have wished to expose herself to the pain of his past, having heard about it too much and too often. Yet she was extraordinarily understanding of his need to speak of the Shoah and she was also proud of the role he had assumed amongst the leaders of the Shoah survivors in Britain.

In the end Roman never went back with my mother and Aviva in the autumn. But his offer to do so was part of a long-established habit of his going on holiday somewhere with my mother and then returning to the same place with his second partner, or vice-versa. It was his peculiar way of being even-handed. Eating in the same restaurants, staying in the same places, in all probability even sleeping in the same bedrooms.

6

RETRACING

Most films featuring a return stick to a chronology, relying on the journey itself to ensure its own narrative and continuity. We accept the fallacy of all such narratives. They purport to retrace the past. "Retrace" – so familiar, so automatic a metaphor. But what does "retrace" mean? Consider its correlative image. What does "retrace" mean? "Retrace" assumes that the past is there to be seen. Yet we were journeying to people and places that, for the most part, could not be seen, places that would yield whatever they had to yield by painful absence.

Not to focus on the discrepancies between perceptions of the past is willingly, perhaps stubbornly, to conform to a fiction: a continuity that can never exist in memory, because neither past nor present is simply continuous, despite our fictive efforts to make it so.

Aloma and I felt uncomfortable with the camera present because it turned what we were experiencing into a kind of performance. For Roman it was very different. The film endowed the journey a higher purpose. He gathered his thoughts, knew what he would say and spoke with disarming directness. The fact that a film of our trip never emerged did not really matter, as this became a dry run for a 20-minute film of him made by Fergal Keane and Fred Scott for the BBC less than a year later which was later crafted into an hour-long film entitled *The Promise*.

Roman was galvanized before the camera. He spoke in clear, pared-down language. Film was an opportunity to bear witness and each time he bore witness it was as though for the first time and to a stranger. He assumed no prior knowledge in his audience, nor did he link what he said to any other words he had said earlier, to any part already filmed. As if he was declaring: "Here it is, direct."

When we were with him he was detached. He saved his energy for communication via the camera. It is interesting that when at home, speaking to family of the Shoah, he talked to us as though to strangers, assuming we knew nothing. In fact, he was more comfortable speaking about his past to strangers – and to us as though we were strangers. What do I mean? His voice only modulated when he spoke to fellow-survivors. They knew. They did not explain to each other. From his viewpoint, family and strangers were equally uninitiated; neither could know, could never truly understand.

Aloma and I shared a general anxiety for our father and the exposure of his raw emotions *there*. I sensed that however often he spoke of the terrible things he witnessed, talking about them in situ would make them different, not only to us, but to him. I hoped it might. I wanted to see and hear a personal side of my father, not the peculiar, impersonal, rehearsed and respected voice, one that was paradoxically so intimate.

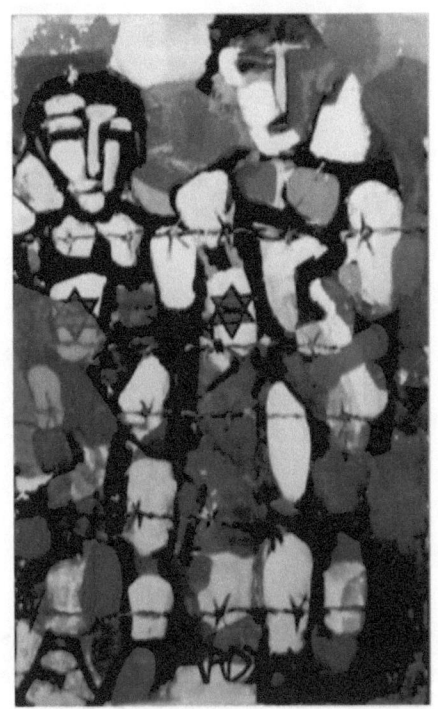

Ghetto Heritage, painting, 1969

7

GHETTO HERITAGE

In 1969 a British Jewish organization advertised a painting competition under the banner "Our Ghetto Heritage". I participated in the up-to-15 age group. The entry form had details, in colour, of a painting by Chagall with a row of shtetl houses and Chagall's version of a cubist face in white, green and black. I had a book on Chagall and loved his colour but was uncomfortable with and scorned his sentimentality. Aged thirteen, I knew little of the history of the ghetto in Europe and had not visited Venice, locus of the prototypical ghetto. For me the word ghetto did not suggest *Yiddishkeit* but separation, incarceration, starvation and eventual death. So my five feet by two-and-a-half foot painting was of two *Katzetniks* with yellow stars behind barbed wire fencing. It won first prize. The lines were black, thick black – the visual vocabulary of Rouault's *Miserere* (I had a copy of Pierre Courtion's beautiful monograph on the artist). The lines were precocious but also too confident, untroubled by their own expression, the angst too easily, readily assumed.

The painting impressed the jurors. What was a boy of 13 doing painting such *Katzetniks*? It drew much attention, and only as I began to receive serious nods of praise did the realization begin to dawn on me that my entry was as false as the competition organisers' invitation to visual *Yiddishkeit*. I had not seen the concentration camps. All I knew were some glimpses in those grim books on my father's shelf. Yet I was praised for a deep seriousness of purpose. Let me be clear about this: my intentions were serious but they were as imprecise as a blunderbuss. What was being perpetuated here? What was my part in it? I had an uneasy feeling that I had too readily assumed the mantle of one entitled to paint that subject. It was as though I had walked down a path that had been laid for me. I could not put my finger on what was not right, but it felt false. My unease was compounded as my parents' friends trooped up the steep steps to the loft to see the painting and nod silently or murmur *sotto voce* praise to my parents.

However, I was not sufficiently discomfited or ashamed to return the 80 pounds in prize money.

8

OIL AND GLASS

Even today the Shoah is an inescapable presence in Europe. It is the nadir, the concentrated expression of the worst in humanity. Those who try and dismiss the Shoah's historical impact do so out of irritation, an irritation expressing a wish that it would go away. But it will not. And the very scale of the annoyance is testimony to the Shoah's impact on history. It has come to such a pitch that it is but a short step to blaming the Jews for their own destruction.

Such is the Shoah's grim unignorability that, as an artist, and one of the Second Generation, I have felt moved over the past 30 years to reflect in paintings, prints, stained-glass or in word, or I've been commissioned to work on projects relating to the Shoah, and genocide. It is not "my subject" but it is a subject to which I have returned.

On reflection, it is clear to me that my own thoughts, the way I form visual ideas, are ligatured to photographs, images, and to received words – be they history or testimony. They were formed by words that formed more words, or images that couple with or overlap other images, composite kernels that, in the creative process of a painting or a stained-glass window, transpose themselves into the work being made. In the course of the realization of an idea, the process of visual creation actually supplants the subject to which it refers. An aesthetic operation is going on, an activity on its own. You are making something and hoping that what you are making might convey the subject as you perceive it. You are making a thing that is an external expression of what one can call, for want of a better word, an idea. And when that idea concerns uncertainty about the possibility of communication, then there are two things: the idea and, like a spacer between you and the subject, a mist of dubiety concerning the idea's communicability.

Oil painting lends itself better than stained glass to express such dubiety, the distance between my experience and the survivor's. In several of the paintings from the series *The Family I Never Knew* I employed lettering, slogans that are suspended, like a veil, between the me/viewer and the subject. These formal devices indicate distance, an abyss I cannot cross, do not wish to cross, the limits to my experience, the distinction between knowledge and inherited knowledge.

Ardyn Halter, Lebensraum, oil on canvas, 1981

Originally there were twelve paintings in this series, all in a scale larger than the viewer (205 x 208 cm) intended to convey a mixed sense of immersion and distance. But there was one that pushed into a nether space of prurience. In it I must have begun to think that I could imagine an experience that was not my own. It ventured onto expressionistic grounds that are not my experience, assuming an angst that is not the emotion of distant bewilderment, but something closer, untrue to my own experience. The emotion wishing to be expressed was real enough to me as I painted it – but not all emotion is true. This earnest emotion was false. My intentions at the time I was painting it counted for nothing because they were confused. I'd stepped quite outside parentheses of doubt. And so I destroyed the painting and did not paint another to replace it. And its absence, for me, in that series represents the labile, fickle nature of assumed experience.

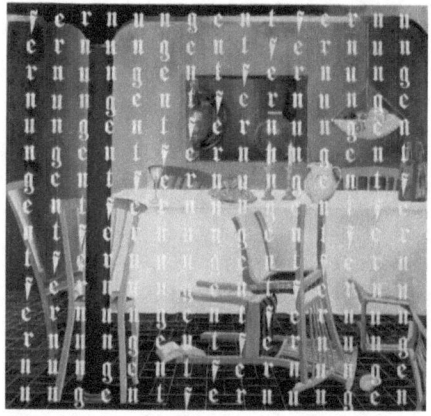

Ardyn Halter, Entfernung *[distancing] oil on canvas, 19..*

Stained glass operates differently from oil painting because it is a medium through which light passes. The great cathedral windows of Europe are "lessons", visual illustrations of the biblical passages read and the sermons preached. They are *solaas*, the palliative to carry the sentence, the moral message.

The projects in stained glass on which I have worked – *Yad LaYeled* the memorial to the one-and-a-half-million Jewish children murdered in the Shoah or the *Beit Midrash*, the prayer hall at St. Johns Wood Synagogue, or the two windows in Kigali that I designed and made to commemorate the Rwandan genocide – were all challenges in communication. For stained glass is a gateway to thought and to emotion. A stained-glass window is not *about* something but *towards* something. It may facilitate, it does not pinpoint thought – for that is the domain of words, pencil or brush. If it communicates, it may do so in part by touching the nervous system, or the pulse of emotion.

9

FROZEN FRAMES OR CONTINUITY

Journeys are well suited to films because of their geographical sequence. Both move in time. In memory our conscious mind struggles to establish the sort of cinematic continuity that tends only to find expression in our subconscious, in the fluidity of dreams. Out of the continuity of our lives memory tends to pluck and recall single moments, images, fragments. This is because moments of thought are also affiliated to or grounded upon moments in memory. "It was there that I realised…." or "It was then that I knew…." We most readily recall frames or specific movement between frames. These are expressed in nugatory words. Then, strangely, memory sometimes reassembles these, like my childhood bus journey, changing their order, constructing new composites.

The advantage of a journey, with stops, watering points, its sequence of meals, conversations, silences, rainy spells, rests, events, is that as a line, however it may meander in space, it forms a continuum, a unity within memory. The journey is the carriage for memory. However aimless, the route, the "deep lane" as T.S. Eliot wrote in *Four Quartets* "insists on the direction/ Into the village".

Something rather peculiar happens when we read a travel book. The journey is the book's carriage and yet, when we think back on what we have read we tend to recall specific scenes, images, sentences. This says something about the process by which images are stored in our brains, by the way in which memory works. Individually and subjectively we deconstruct what we have seen, particularising and atomising experience. The telling scenes do not offer themselves to us chronologically but as islands in an uncharted, random archipelago.

So, with the slippage of time, memory would in all likelihood distil this journey to a few particular impressions. And these, in time, would likely shrink to moments, to a few images. In comparison to a film such nuggets seem less "real". For the presence of a film urgently claims: "This is how it was. This is more true, more real than the unreliability of memory."

Our physical journey to Poland would be like so many other journeys taken by survivors along with their children, the Second Generation, back to the towns, *shtetls*, ghettos, concentration camps, forests, the places of killing and dying, the places of chance escape – locations connected to rare moments of kindness or particular brutality. These routes have been charted by thousands of families. They are all similar and yet no two are the same.

Just as a survivor may be impelled, driven by a need at some point, however late in his or her life, to confront the past, so too many of the Second Generation feel a similar impulse. The past is like a shadow stretching long in the late afternoon sun to where you are standing.

10

RWANDA – WHY RWANDA?

In the early summer of 2003, my father and I were asked to submit designs for two stained-glass windows for the projected national genocide memorial in Rwanda which was due to open in the spring of 2004. The organisers had seen the stained-glass windows we had made for *Yad LaYeled* at the Ghetto Fighters' Museum in Israel. A high proportion of the Rwandan people are churchgoers. Rwandan society is over 90 per cent Christian (roughly half are Roman Catholic, one quarter Protestant and between ten and 15 per cent Adventist) with fairly high church attendance. Many of the churches in Rwanda, however modest, have some simple stained-glass elements. Therefore it was thought that the visual presence of stained glass in the national genocide memorial would be fitting. Two large windows in the main building, each measuring about 3.00 x 2.50 metres at the central memorial exhibit had been detailed for the stained glass.

"It's a huge project," my father said. "They are short on time and will never complete it."

"Surely that is not our problem," I answered, "but it is an important project and we can complete our part. Whether they have the building done in time for an opening date isn't really relevant to us. It is worthy. The project must be done. And I think we should be associated with it."

"You have no idea what you would be getting into here," said my father. "They will never raise the funds. We won't get paid and more than half a year of work and materials will have been wasted. Nothing will come of it. I am telling you now, I will have nothing to do with this."

I replied that with the organisers' strength of will they would succeed – after all, they had, as a family, created the first Holocaust memorial centre in the United Kingdom, near Nottingham, while the Jewish community in Britain had done little but talk about one. But, so far as I was concerned, that was the lesser point. The key issue was that there are two lessons to learn from the Shoah. The first is vigilance. Words can become deeds, so one should never assume that the virus of anti-Semitism won't recur. The second is that Jews, as a people, must be sensitive to the persecution of other minorities.

I argued: "If you, a survivor, and I, from the Second Generation, do not care, then who should?"

"This is different from the Shoah," my father said. "There have been wars and killings throughout African history."

"And throughout European history. This was a genocide," I replied. "All genocides are different. They differ in scale but they are essentially the same. They result from one section of the people, a race, a minority, a religion, being dehumanized, persecuted and butchered. Surely you can see that. Almost a million people were murdered in Rwanda. They were killed with machetes and clubs and bullets and not with Zyklon gas. The methods were not industrial but this was genocide. We should be involved."

"I've already told you," my father repeated. "I will have nothing to do with this. I am having nothing to do with this project."

That last sentence was familiar. He had said it in the self-same place in his studio-loft only a few years before. We had been asked to design and make a stained-glass window for the prayer room, the *Beit Midrash* of St Johns Wood Synagogue in London, the place where *shaharit*, the morning prayers, and the Talmud *gemara* lessons were conducted. We agreed to work on the project together. But who would design it?

"We will both submit designs and the one they choose will be the one we will make," Roman had said. Such openness disarmed my worries that competition might cause. "If you win, I'll assist you and if I win you will assist me." I readily agreed to this.

In the St Johns Wood Synagogue project the rubric was very difficult, almost impossible. They wanted the window to commemorate four themes: Shoah and Rebirth; Torah and Talmud; The State of Israel and, alongside these great themes, the tragic death in a ski accident of a member of their community, the sister-in-law of the donor. How could these vastly differing themes be reconciled within one stained-glass image?

Roman decided for some reason that the 3.5 x 2.5 metre window should only have stained glass in the centre and plain glass sections around it. So, in his largely abstract design, the stained glass itself would measure only about 1.5 metres x 1.0 metres.

My design was for a Tree of Life to encompass the entire window, with sombre blues, green and indigo at the base rising to optimistic colours at the top. Above the tree were the words that are sung when the Torah is put back into the ark: "It is a tree of life to its adherents; those who follow it find happiness." Loss, growth, memory, study.

My design was accepted and I consulted with Jumbo Robinson at the foundry in Essex to discuss the casting since I needed to know that my design was technically practical. I had to ascertain that the molten aluminium would run well along the fine filigree, the thin lines that ran in counterpoint to the broader structural branches, that these points would not create air pockets or block in the casting. Jumbo gave me the thumbs up.

When Roman came to see my fully enlarged design he looked at it long and in silence before declaring: "All those thin lines won't cast. This is a shitty design. I am having nothing to do with this project." Shocked by the venom of his reaction I was left wondering if this was pique or the tone of architectural crits from back in his days in the early 1950s when he had been a student at the Architectural Association.

He did nothing more on the project except, as a sort of palliative afterthought, he arranged for a carved dedication to the donor's sister-in-law, Anabelle Paradise, in steamed oak that sat across the windowsill inside the Beit Midrash, beneath the window. But because the project had been given to us both to make I put his initials beside mine on the stained glass. This was naively altruistic.

Now, accustomed to my father's outbursts of rage, and aware that they were so often induced by a sudden drop in his blood sugar, here, on the Rwanda project I made a second attempt.

"Join me on this."

I felt bewildered. Had my father reached his quantum of pain? It was as though the cup of horror was full and there was no space left within him to accommodate the suffering of others.

"At the very least, say you will voice support," I said.

He was silent.

"I am going to make the window," I said.

My father shrugged and gestured to say: "It's up to you." He shook his head and walked down the steep stairs from the loft studio.

One of the 50 sections making up the two stained-glass windows for the National Genocide Memorial in Rwanda.

11

WHO CARES?

So I completed the designs, they were photographed and emailed to Aegis Trust who emailed them to the Rwandan National Genocide Memorial Center's key backers in Sweden, the Netherlands, and the UK's department for International Development and The Clinton Foundation. (The 1994 genocide had been perpetrated during Bill Clinton's presidency and he had been gripped by a sense of guilt that it had happened on his watch, that he failed to respond and by the time the slow wheels of administrative action had begun to turn, the hundred days of feverish slaughter were done and close to a million mostly Tutsi men, women and children had been murdered by the Hutu militias). Within a week I received e-approval for my design. Now I had to work day and night to make the windows in time for the opening in April 2004.

At the end of March 2004 I completed the windows, each in 25 sections, assisted during a week of that time by my sister Aviva Halter-Hurn. It was fortifying to receive help within the family, even for a few days. I had crates constructed, lining the wood on all sides with thick cushions of polystyrene, for if any pane broke in transit there would be absolutely nothing one could do out there in Rwanda. At that time almost nothing could be purchased locally. It would be impossible to take replacement panes of glass in every colour of those windows. The ten crates were collected and I watched them be loaded onto a truck and prayed that they might arrive intact. They were shipped from Heathrow to Brussels to Nairobi, to Kigali and then taken on trucks to Gisozi, the hill outside the Rwandan capital designated as the site for the National Genocide Memorial. In April I flew out to Rwanda to assemble the windows. I was very apprehensive. Would the shipment arrive? And would the windows get there smashed? Yet I was also apprehensive since my first journey to a place of genocide would be to the land of another people's genocide. When a year later we were in Poland, I found that thoughts of Rwanda interwove with what I heard and saw. The methods of genocide were different and the timescale too, 100 days compared to six years of war. In Rwanda the genocide was mostly conducted piecemeal, using machetes, clubs, flames and bullets, the largest mass killings occurring when congregations were massed in their wooden churches and the buildings set on fire. The Shoah, by contrast, was the systematic industrialization of death. Yet in my mind the threads interwove.

"Why?" you may ask. "Why? It is another's experience. You couldn't feel it in the same way. You are presuming."

Well, that is probably true. But then my father's experience was also "another's", across a distance I cannot bridge, and my experience as son-of, Second Generation, whatever one calls it, may to you be just that same distance. Is the death of one stranger different to the death of another? A different colour skin. Black strangers and not family, my uncles, aunts, cousins, grandparents, great-grandparents, yet all were strangers. I just happen to have inherited genetic characteristics of the latter group.

I wanted to accept the commission to work on the Rwandan Genocide Memorial project *because* my family were murdered in another genocide. If I did not care, who would?

12

CROSSING A LINE

In 2012 my father died. In 2014 The Ben Uri Museum/Gallery in London held a retrospective show of his work. The director David Glasser and I worked closely on this. He sought an appropriate focus. How should Roman Halter's life work be seen as an artist? He mulled this over for some time. The show and the book would in no small measure determine the nature of my father's legacy. *Through stained-glass* – was David Glasser's inspired decision. After all, Roman had considered his large paintings as designs for stained glass, so let that be the approach. David and his curator Thomas Hughes pressed ahead and I was on tap during the year of preparation with emails, photos, answers and support. One thing frustrated and irritated me. Time and again David Glasser told me that Roman's name was associated with the stained-glass windows in Rwanda. He kept harping back on this. "It's all over the internet, Ardyn. There are newspaper interviews. Take a look." It took four or five lengthy emails to persuade him that this was simply erroneous.

The day after the opening of the exhibition, my sister Aviva and I decided to sort through three more boxes of his papers and letters in the basement of the family house in Crouch End, London. In the third box I chanced upon the following letter to him from the head of an Oxford college, dated April 2004 – about two weeks after I had shipped out the 10 crates of stained-glass windows, and as I was about to leave or was en-route to Rwanda.

Dear Roman,

How good to hear your news. How admirable that you have taken on the stained-glass windows in Rwanda. It must be wonderful to be able to involve your son and daughter in a project like this. I look forward to seeing photos of the work...

With best greetings, David

I sat down, reeling. Just imagine you have written a book, working day and night for seven months only to discover that your name on the cover has been replaced by your father's. A book, a stained-glass window, a symphony... what is the difference?

My father's words echoed repeatedly in my head: "I will have nothing to do with this project." And my own: "At the very least... voice support."

When Johann Strauss, the father, hired men to boo his son Richard Georg's concert, hostility was overt. This was very different. "At the very least... voice support." This was not support but annexation. Take away the name of an artist from his work and what is left? And now it might seem that I, seeking to rectify my father's appropriation of my work, was trying to appropriate his work.

Presumably the same sort of letter to which this was a response had gone out to many, many others. My father was a serial letter-writer, penning hand-written notes in his beautiful sepia-ink italic script. Indeed, a couple of years later, I came upon a similar letter of praise to him from the Chief Rabbi Lord Sacks for undertaking this worthy project. Once again, I felt gutted.

During 2013 and 2014 a good deal of my time had been spent ensuring his reputation, the memorial exhibition, the hard-back book.

How admirable that you have taken on the stained-glass windows in Rwanda. It must be wonderful to be able to involve your son and daughter in a project like this.

And there was nothing I could say to him. He was dead. How had he seen it? Did he regard everything he had created as part of him? From the loins of, as in from the studio of.... I sat on the bench in the stube – the dining room in my parents' house, leaning on the planed-down door that was the table, close to where he had once sat.

How had he permitted himself to lay claim to work that was not his but mine? I fancy that he blurred the boundary in his mind, from opposition to support, from support to participation, from participation to pride, from pride to annexation, representing my work as his. He had stepped across a line and one part of me would never forgive him. Another part felt love and the two could not be reconciled.

After the frustrations of rage waned, I could only smile.

13

ALOMA'S CHALLENGE

For Aloma, my sister, our trip to Poland would be a necessary stage in a gargantuan task she had undertaken, editing the 1,400 page autobiography of our father's experiences between 1939 and 1945. Hers was the unenviable task of wrestling between versions, cross-checking, testing my father's memory against what he had written, to clarify and edit it. She sought to protect the writer – all the more so her father – from his own lacunae and slips. In the main, her questions were met by irritation bordering on aggression, as if she was challenging the very fibre of his being.

His method was to laboriously pen each draft by hand, have the manuscript typed, photocopy the latest draft, sometimes penning further changes to the typescript. More often than not, he photocopied that amended version. And then, before sending out the photocopy, he sometimes added further notes on top of it. Or having sent out a photocopy, he then revised only the copy he held, leaving my sister to edit a chapter that was not, in fact, the most updated one.

He filed the different versions undated, and seemed reluctant ever to throw away earlier drafts. This may have been physical proof to himself of his fidelity to his own promise to remember, record, tell. Or he may simply have feared losing what was written. Keep everything, everything until the book is ready. The material was chaotic. Aloma said it was the most difficult book in her professional editing career.

Aloma's professionalism met with brusque authoritarian tones. Roman was never intrigued by the historicity of memory, the way his mind had affected controlled release of information over the decades. Unconsciously, his own father Max's patriarchal habits, as he had reported them to us, found expression when he himself was close to his home environment. He demanded honour, respect, attention, and compliance. So for my sister, the journey was mostly unpleasant and also wounding. Silent anger was always the most potent weapon in his arsenal.

14

INCOMPLETE

The first film of the journey was never completed. It would have been typical of my father in a characteristically expansive moment to offer – and then later regret – to help in approaching potential sponsors for the film. We never saw any of the material filmed. Close to a year went by. No film emerged. Then Roman declared he was going back to Poland without us and with Fergal Keane, the acclaimed BBC TV reporter and independent documentary filmmaker, Fred Scott, at the camera and Poppy Segag-Montefiore. That film was produced and edited within just two weeks of their return, with a discipline and focus of film coverage for news reporting. It was called *Roman's Journey* – the same title Aloma had given to his book, published by Portobello Books in 2007 (republished in 2023 by Amsterdam Publishers). The film was twenty minutes long and was screened over half a dozen times on BBC4 and the World Service in 2006-7.

Several months before we went to Poland with Mark Hirsch, Roman asked me if I thought we should go with him or with Fergal Keane. It was clear, I suggested, that Fergal Keane would make the better film. Besides, he'd likely experience less difficulty finding funding, and he had an open door at the BBC. I had met Fergal in Rwanda on the long day of the official opening of the National Genocide Memorial Centre, as we waited for the endless motorcades of successive African leaders to arrive, in a form of reverse pecking order, the last being perceived as the most important, since all the others would have to attend his arrival. As we were waiting tedious hours for the leaders to arrive, and the invited survivors were wilting in the humidity, Fergal said, "Let me tell you. Your father... He's one of the few people I have time for in this world."

Halter house in Chodecz

15

SNAPSHOTS

I have just been looking back on the snapshots of our journey to Poland. The photos yield next to nothing. They never even made it into an album. They were bland; they do not show what I saw. They have little or nothing to do with what I remember and felt then. They reinforce a tangible vacancy.

What we see on a journey (and the changes affected to that journey with the passage of time), as stored in our minds, is impossible for us to evaluate. It is as fluid as a stream. Nothing stays still, even though we think it does. The only exception to this is trauma, which remains what and where it is.

To view a painting in an exhibition there before your eyes and to see it in memory are two very different things. If I can recall the order of almost every painting I have seen in exhibitions, (and I state this not to boast but as a point of fact and also because this type of memory is not really all that advantageous), because positioning it spatially in the gallery spaces or museums within my mind, this still does not mean that I can *see* those paintings. Beside which, even if I could, and

I cannot, each time we *see* a painting (see, rather than recognize the presence of) we are seeing something different, because we *are* constantly different and we, the light, the day, our feelings, our lives have all changed. Nothing is the same, but in flux.

16

GRANDPARENTS ON PAPER

Round about the time my father painted the watercolour of the men in the forest (I was about seven years old) he also painted a sombre watercolour, similar in style, on thick paper with a rough deckle edge. There were two people, their faces emerging out of a deep burnt-umber and sepia gloom. The contours of their features were in thick black lines and they looked sadder than the hieratic long-nosed icons in his book on Byzantine art. When I asked him who they were he told me, "My parents". I knew that they were not alive. They never sent me postcards on my birthday like Grandma Bertha from Budapest. I could also sense that father did not wish me to question him further.

In 1965 when I was nine, and Aloma was eleven, our parents took us to the Georges Rouault exhibition at The Tate Gallery. Christ's anguish in the *Miserere*, the faces of the judges and many of the prostitutes and clowns spoke the same expressionist sadness as that watercolour image of my grandparents. In Georges Rouault's canvases rich cobalt and vermillion glinted vividly through black and grey shadow, reminding me of the intense colour flashing through centuries' grime of cathedral stained-glass we had seen that summer in Chartres and Rheims. Whereas my father's watercolour seemed withdrawn, pulled into the depths of its sepia and black, Rouault's works tapped into a continuum, a mournful flowing river that was painful, brutalized, and yet still beautiful.

My grandparents, as painted by my father, looked to me like faces long lost. They seemed like people of whom nothing more could be said. What was painted there prevented further expression. He framed that painting shortly after completing it and hung it in the apartment corridor. Behind the glass they seemed still further removed. I *saw* neither them, nor a clear reflection of myself in the glass. They could not have seemed further away.

The common ground between the two, my father and Rouault, was a sense that painting was both painful and necessary. Stylistically, my father's painting tapped into both expressionism and Byzantine iconography. Both pared human life down to something essential. They bared the raw core whilst also blocking so much, reducing the image through the sheer weight of line.

"Il a été maltraité et opprimé et il n'a pas ouvert la bouche."

Georges Rouault, Miserere

17

INNER SCREENS

Primo Levi wrote *If This Is A Man* just two years after the war in 1947, at the age of 28 whilst working in his profession as a chemist, at DUCO, a Dupont paint factory outside Torino. He was exceptional as a writer and differed from the younger survivors in that so soon after his liberation he recorded his experiences of concentration camp life in Auschwitz/Buna in dispassionate detail. Few of the younger survivors, like my father, for whom concentration camps and slave labour had been their high schooling returned to live in their country of birth. They had to learn a new language, start afresh, gain a profession, build a life.

My father could not write or relate his experiences until much later. And when he did, they were not expressed in sequential narrative but in scenes that he wrote and rewrote. He began this in the early 1960s dictating these memoirs to my mother. She had arrived in London with the Hungarian Olympic swimming squad in 1948, remained with her aunt and uncle in a grand house on a leafy road in Crouch End, on a hill with a commanding view of the city. She enrolled on a brief shorthand course before working as secretary to the manager of the London office of Air India. This was a time when a main office had no more than a single telephone line and the duties of a secretary seldom exceeded one or two letters dictated in the course of a morning. She later confided to us that she could not always transcribe what she had taken down in dictation. What commenced with occasional dictation to my mother behind closed doors (*nicht für die Kinder* – they spoke German to each other when they did not want us to understand) became a daily activity of remembering.

In time my father came to speak openly about his past even to, especially to strangers. It was as though his mind was a castle with many gates and with each passing decade another gate opened, permitting his past to emerge. Such was his trauma – it was as if those mental portcullises existed in order to protect him from what he had lived through and enabled him, immediately after the war, to inhabit the world of normality. They protected the inner keep but in his heart the trauma could never be worked out, rationalised or "dealt with". And those gates delayed the process by which my father externalised his experience. Eventually, once they were all open, the protection was gone and his nights and days were absorbed in reflection on the Shoah. It shadowed him. Even when he swam – and he loved swimming – he would say *Amachai* (a Yiddish word, from the Hebrew *mechayeh*, "revive, to provide life-force", in my father's use would be "how life-giving, how marvellous") and in that word *Amachai*, propelling its pleasure upward was the contrast with the shadow, its opposite, the bourne of comparison for everything in his life.

18

ANOMALOUS

Of all destinations for winter holidays my parents chose Austria – the Tyrol. This went on for several years, Christmas and Easter, until the après-ski incident.

Austria was not the first choice – once before we went on a family ski vacation to the stylish resort of Megève. After three days there my parents had spent what they intended to in a week, so they bought a primus stove and small frying pan and cooked in the room of the *pension* where we stayed. So with budget in mind, the following year they opted for the Tyrol and we took the boat train and Arlberg Express sleeping on overnight couchettes. The following morning, liking the snows they saw, we descended at Otztal, and took an ancient taxi to the highest hamlet in Austria where deep snow smothered the roofs and the sweet earthy scent of hay and cattle issued from the barns. The atmosphere was simple, yokelish, *gemütlich* and the prices very low. The pound Sterling bought abundant Austrian schillings.

We went to Obergurgl despite the fact that the Tyrolean valleys had been a recruiting ground of the SS seeking the fit young Alpine stock, and stayed above the hamlet, in fact looking down on it from a commanding location. Three stone three-story barrack buildings had been built as an SS training centre in 1939. Today these are affiliated to the University of Innsbruck. Later, years later, one summer with no snow cloaking the graves, I noted that there was not a single male grave from the war years. All must have perished on the Eastern front. So why did we go there, and why did we return? Was it because Nazism had been defeated? Did my parents feel it was a new and different world? Or were we there because they felt they had a right to enjoy the loveliness of such places and that, by being there, they could assert – in their hearts – that they had survived? Or was it simply a matter of the favourable rate of exchange?

Winter sports were still dependent on local craft. Old Riml sewed the ski boots with inner and outer lacing. Ski poles were made of bamboo or wood with metal and leather baskets, and skis were hickory wooden with metal tips.

Ski lifts were single-seater and so slow that on the high lifts poncho-style blankets were given to the skiers so they would not perish from hypothermia by the time they reached the top.

We stayed in the Haus Kuraten, a lovely old wooden chalet with low ceilings, an ancient pine-panelled *Stube* and not a right angle in the whole building. The steps sloped, the floor creaked and the knotty pine was hand-planed, broad panelled and knotted. The curate was a sprightly bald man, patron of the ski school. Frau Scheiber ran the house, an indefatigable *Hausfrau*, she was kindly and welcoming to everyone. At the end of a day's skiing one was greeted by the smell of hot butter *Kuchen* baked on her Aga, dusted with powder sugar.

The inhabitants of the Otztaler Alps are devout Catholics and the Haus Kuraten was exemplary. Every corner of every room had a carved crucifix, and the middle of some of the walls had an extra one for good measure. There were more crucifixes than there were pegs to hang coats or ski clothes to dry. The stigmata were not just carved. They were painted in blood red. And to lend the tragic story verisimilitude, beneath the effigies of the crucified Christ with drops of blood were painted mini-splashes on the linen chest or on the panelled floor. I cannot recall any carvings of the devil but at the foot of the Steinmann lift, on the David Hutte, there was a fresco of St. Bernhard with his foot firmly grounded on the neck of the devil, whose face was that of a stereotypical Jew, straight out of *Der Stürmer*.

It was here, in the Haus Kuraten, that we as a family celebrated Hanukkah. The curtains were drawn. Towels or shirts were draped over the crucifixes to prevent Him from witnessing the celebration of the Hasmonean uprising. The Hanukkiah was lit and sotto voce we sang *Maoz Zur*.

I do remember thinking it peculiar that my parents did not find this strange.

Our times in Obergurgl ended with a misunderstanding. After a long day's skiing my father and I just made it to the bottom of the Gaisberg chairlift to take one last ride up before the lift closed. On our single seats, we were about 15 feet off the ground when we passed the Jenewein Hotel where a group, kirsch flasks in hand, celebrating the end of a happy day's skiing stood in a neat circle, lifted their right legs to 90 degrees, and shouted out "*Schi Heil! Schi Heil! Schi Heil!!*"

On the chairlift I was one seat ahead of my father and turned round to watch the revellers. It was then that I saw my father on the chair behind. His face had turned white. He seemed contemplating jumping to the piste below but he was too high off the ground. He shouted something but the laughing and cheering men did not hear or notice him. Of course long before we reached the top the men had dispersed and though my father skied down madly to find them they were gone.

"Did you hear them shouting *Sieg Heil?*" he said to me when I caught up with him at the bottom of the run.

"They shouted *Schi Heil!*" I returned. But it made no difference. We headed back in silence to the Haus Kuraten.

The following year we skied in Switzerland, in Zermatt.

19

INVOLVING THE NEXT GENERATION

Writing his book, my father was impelled by a tremendous sense of urgency, and when he enlisted our help in editing, he presented this as though it was not to help him so much as posterity. He phoned to tell us the particular chapter had been posted. He expected immediate attention but never mentioned that he was sending both of us the same text to edit. It was bad enough to re-read each draft knowing we had already edited earlier versions, let alone discover that we were duplicating each other's work. And there was the inescapable foreboding that there would always be another draft, more detailed than the last. We could not bring ourselves to decline the task.

Inevitably, the presence of his memory interposed over an extended period into our own biographical memories. This is sensed by many of the "second generation" and begs the question whether the atrocities of the past increase one's historical awareness, in a general way, or infiltrate themselves more like the cuckoo of another's memory within your nest.

Finally, in 2005, after so many years, the Sisyphean task was over. *Roman's Journey* was out, completed. Now at last there would be no more versions.

Yet our father was possessed by the sense that there were more details he could tell which had to be said. No published account could ever be satisfactory. After publication he felt guilty about the people excluded in the scenes Aloma had edited out. And he voiced this to friends. Although he knew it had to be done, he found it hard to accept. The telling would always be incomplete.

20

AVALANCHE

Looking back, Roman often wondered in disbelief at having survived the experience that he held in his memory. Shadowing this was the fear that if he himself could scarcely believe it, then how could others?

An off-piste skier riding the glinting white powder after a heavy fresh fall in late March traverses a steep couloir, then after only a few turns hears an unmistakable lateral crack across the mountain. It penetrates his consciousness like the opening of a door you hear in your sleep. He senses the slipping mass of snow undermining his own descent, then hears the light echo of the snow-wave turn to a growl, driving all before it, as it scoops and tosses the stricken skier like a rag doll whipped over and over. The thunder of white blasts his matchstick skis dozens of metres away and then, quite by chance, flicks the skier in the air clear of the main wave, whilst the avalanche moves on below tearing rocks and trees until its force is spent. The skier looks about bewildered at the torn line: trees smashed, the ground stripped in its wake. He lives to tell the tale but can never describe the force he has encountered and survived, the utter helplessness. Henry Schlee, a powerfully built friend of mine, described this to me. It happened to him off-piste on Mont Gelé in Verbier, in Switzerland. The avalanche tumbled him six or seven hundred metres before throwing him to the surface. An articulate man, he was unable to find words to describe the experience and as he spoke, his eyes and his gestures conveyed one thing: that nothing he said could ever communicate what he had been through, the force, or his helplessness.

"You are always told that if you are ever caught in an avalanche, you should make swimming, breaststroke-movements with your arms... swim to the surface. *Swim to the surface*.... ! The forces around you are unimaginable."

21

SHOAH – SOME DEFINITIONS

Shoah is the Hebrew for a blazing wind of fire, a force leaving in its wake a swathe of destruction. *Shoah*, single form. *Sho'ot*, plural form. There have been other *sho'ot* in Jewish experience. The Hebrew word *shoah* appears 13 times in the bible in the book of Job, Psalms, Proverbs, Ezekiel and Zaphaniah (several times in each of these). The meanings of *shoah* in the Bible encompass many facets of destruction: ruin; desolation; a huge crash; a whirlwind; a storm; the power of the sword; ravages. In the past there have been other *sho'ot*. *Shoah* is the term the Jewish people have come to adopt to describe the destruction of European Jewry (preferable to the word Holocaust with its sacrificial overtones and its unavoidable claims of exclusivity).

Until the Shoah, an event like the bombing of Dresden might have been classified as a *shoah*.

22

TIME TO TELL

At home, or indeed anywhere, once the subject of the Shoah entered a conversation, the balance shifted. Dialogue became an account that could not be interactive because the experience was one-sided. Typically, over a meal, once he raised the subject my father would pause mid-sentence to take a bite. Such sustaining bites acted as an unconscious technique of suspense in the way that a mild stutter compels polite attention. The combination of a person relating Shoah experiences whilst eating might seem singularly inappropriate to some people. Bite, mastication and swallow were pauses, they spun out the telling, and the relish of table became in a bizarre way linked to his relish in talking. It was the tone of appetite that I always found singularly unsettling, even embarrassing. It always seemed that there ought to be a manner, a demeanour more suited to this subject, something akin to the tone of Primo Levi's writing: lucid, precise, through which one glimpses unimaginable pain, a distance which at the same time communicates a dreadful engagement. This subject seemed to me to be one unsuited to the table or even to daily ease and family warmth – too appalling to slip across between courses. Often I felt close to expressing this but checked my words. Were my feelings merely stock bourgeois etiquette? Who am I to judge? Why should my father conform to a prudish humility that I might consider appropriate? The very act of eating was an assertion of his survival.

But why did he need to assert it in this way? And to this I find no clear single answer. It was bewildering, almost miraculous to him when he reflected on what he lived through. Endlessly, an inner voice repeated: *you have survived*. Those events seemed nearly impossible to him. His telling was an assertion of strength and a wellspring of pain, at times of guilt, or grief or the sense of a chasm that for him would never close. These are historical facts, these are the appalling details and *I have lived through them, I am here, telling*. With the passing of time, the more incredible it seemed to him that he lived through the Shoah.

Besides the numb astonishment at what he survived, he was also cheering himself up, affirming the life coursing through him like a green fuse despite all odds. Yet, perhaps it was at those moments when he felt most alive that he was reminded of the opposite. Food reminded him of starvation, pleasure of loss and at those moments, seemingly apropos of nothing he would begin to recount a memory. Since we talk about what we are doing or what is on our minds, he talked about the Shoah.

Apart from the faces of his parents and of the men in the forest, he set down his experiences on canvas in a series of works in the 1970s. In 2006 they were exhibited in Tate Britain and now seven of those paintings are in the permanent collection of The Imperial War Museum. In the last five years of his life he set out to record them visually for a second time. He painted his dreams, mostly columns of tiny figures, men, women, children – minute, spikey, scarcely distinguishable groups or columns being marched to their deaths, superimposed over gentle watercolours of Dorset. The juxtaposition of gentle rural England with details of genocidal atrocities is shocking, disturbing. Is this what he saw when he painted the grass-cloaked chalk hills between Birdsmoorgate and Bridport? Or was he dissatisfied by the simple calm of the pastoral watercolours? Were they too gently anodyne, too disconnected from what he carried within him? Was that why he began to superimpose his Shoah memories on the watercolours? And was that also why he called them dreams? Dreams that were not confined to the night.

It is only really possible to know what is going on in those small paintings by reading the inscription scripted beneath each one in his fine calligraphy. For example: (beneath a scene of hills in gentle viridian, washing into ochre, beneath a blue sky, whose contour is broken by trees in silhouette, or are they trees?)

"Mothers and children being marched to be shot."

Or "A nightmare of children taken from their homes and led down to the quarry between the trees by the lake."

Roman Halter, Death march, watercolour

23

RWANDA NOTES 1 : CIRCLING

The wooden frames, the structures that will carry my stained-glass windows, have been prepared in advance of my arrival according to the size and plan I sent. In their zeal to improve upon the design, the local Rwandan carpenters have routed out the inner corner of each frame section. However, this recess needed to be simple and square since it is exactly where the screws that will hold each section of stained glass – 25 sections for each window – will bite into the hardwood frame. So these zealous unsolicited additional labours now need to be filled in.

Whilst discussing this with John, the Rwandan carpenter, I found myself looking at his blunt saw, its teeth like rounded molars, his hand-plane, a Stanley that must be 20 years old if it is a day, its blade worn to a dull angle, no glue, and a box of bent masonry nails. These were his tools, the full set.

A young girl or woman – hard to tell her age – crouched in the corner of the building outside the hardwood frame that we were trying to fix. A Prussian-blue scarf was tied over her hair. She had a small bucket and brush. Her eyes were timid, like a young doe. John is a Tutsi in his early fifties with quick, smiling eyes. He told me that the girl's name is Violette. She is eighteen or nineteen years old. Her parents, brothers and sisters were killed in the 1994 genocide. So she was a little girl of eight at the time of the genocide. She appeared afraid – or disturbed.

"John, is she is alright?" Alright. Aware as soon as I uttered the word how meaningless it is. John said he knows her, knew her family and she is the only member to have survived. She was raised by distant relatives, and by friends of her parents who survived. He said he has been keeping an eye on her. Today she has seen the son and brother of the man who butchered her family. They were working with the plasterers, round the corner on the south side of the building. Violette stayed close to us, we on the inside of the open window frame, she on the outside. When the plasterers passed by, carrying sacks of cement on their shoulders, I looked for her but she was not there. Minutes later she had mysteriously reappeared. It was hard to tell quite what work she was engaged to do but she appeared busy.

In the mid-afternoon, when I finally realised there could be no further progress on the frame today, for the wood battens were only promised for the following morning, I took a taxi back and sat on the terrace of the Intercontinental Hotel, by the pool in which only I ever seemed to swim in. The waiter asked me for my order the moment I sat down, and I felt obliged to order, even though I really only wanted to just sit there.

Thinking about Violette, I stopped stirring my cup, the milk didn't want to blend with the tea, and watched the ripples settle I saw something, a speck, like a small leaf, a few tones darker than the liquid, moving across it and turning, slowly. Another similar speck entered the white porcelain circle at 90 degrees to the first. As I watched their progress I saw that they could not be leaves but reflections. Glancing up to the open sky I saw a dozen eagles with massive wingspans, circling on the afternoon thermals overhead, over my head. I began to wonder if they could all be interested in the small sandwiches, or perhaps in me. The aerial survey made me uncomfortable but I did not move. The threat seemed so improbable. The twelve eagles were joined by several others, winding in, one by one, into the hub.

Did Violette see her family macheted? What did she remember?

She would have been only two or three years younger than my father when, through the cover of trees and bushes, he saw his Jewish school-friends clubbed, bayoneted and shot by their former classmates, keen young SS recruits. It was in the shallow quarry near the lake of Chodecz where they all used to play when they were younger. Of course Violette remembers everything. She is now eighteen or so. My father would have been 22 or 23, ten years after he saw that first atrocity. Ten years on. Ten years. What is ten years? An Iliad decade, or a mere 3,000 individual days?

The reflected eagles circled in my tea like those black mole-matt speck figures projected in Michal Rovner's *Culture Plates* – Petri dishes that she exhibited at the Venice Biennale. Her version of human ovens in the snow was also projected on a wall in thickly blotched monochrome, a circle of people, forever turning, the outermost now inside, the inner ones moving out, flesh skin warming flesh skin, something my father had done on *Appel* in Stutthof, wearing nothing more than their striped shirts at dawn in the freezing Baltic winter. And Rovner's *Culture Plate* figures showed bird's eye views of head and shoulders, as though you are looking down from a high balcony onto people moving around a city square in the snow, like the dancing figures in the YouTube video of Gary Jules's song *Mad World*.

And I – what am I to them? Do eagles see in black and white or colour? Yes, of course, all birds see in colour. So, from two or three-hundred feet above, with their needle-sharp vision, my head would appear like a target, pink where my hair is thinning, circled in brown and then a white shirt, over the tea-table. No more than a speck of promise, nourishment to the circling birds above me on this verandah. Unless, that is, as they circle they build up a full picture, a highly precise image of me, a three-dimensional imaged matrix. What would the eagle's summary be? Would it be reduced to a simplification: moving flesh or carrion?

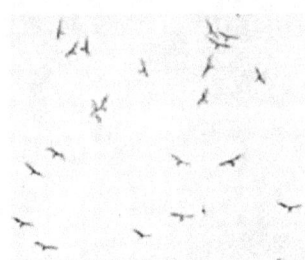

24

PATRIARCHAL

When we were visiting Poland, Roman related how his father, my grandfather, ruled the home. Max Mordechai Halter was a figure of absolute patriarchal authority, brooking no dissent, yet constantly challenged by his children. His second son Pesach, Peccio, ran away from home in his early teens. He wanted to go to Palestine. He was a Zionist. He was brought back from the border (his father had alerted the police to look for Peccio). Max wanted Peccio to be a Torah scribe because he had beautiful handwriting but Peccio was adventurous, tried to run away to Paris, to Africa, to Palestine and then rebelled when, like his elder brother Shlomo, he chose his own bride. Max harboured resentment, as though his eldest sons had done this not out of love but to spite his authority. So Max did not attend either of the weddings, and his sons did not bring their brides to the family home. Instead of pooling their energies as a family they squandered them in separate rancour while the Nazi wave that threatened them swelled and loomed.

Despite this consciousness of his own father's pent-up ire and authoritarianism, my father reacted towards Mark Hirsch and June Kent and to my sister and me in almost as imperious a way. It was as though his wheels were now locked to a rail gauge he neither wished nor was able to change. Questions were parried as personal challenges. In Poland, stressed by the visit, in the presence of memories of his own father, there in the house his father had built, in the place of his childhood, or later in Lodz, Auschwitz, Krakow or Dresden, he seemed to become like his own father. If we asked him a question, however simple, or sought to match what he was saying against what we had heard from his lips in the past, merely in order to clarify matters in our minds or to reconcile discrepant versions, he would react sharply. Whatever the question, he would begin his response with: "No..." even if in his reply he went on to agree. He was not conscious of this. It puzzled us. Perhaps we should have told him. It might have diffused his tension. He had no mental space for the distraction of our presence; the past was overwhelming him and we felt uncomfortable, almost guilty being with him.

25

NECESSARY SPACE

At the height of his professional career as an architect, when he must have been in his mid-to-late thirties or early forties, I recall my father as a man of intense activity. A Spartan start to the day involved us rising early – a jog round Hampstead Heath and Kenwood, followed by a swim in the men's bathing pond. We drove quickly home for breakfast and then I'd be dropped off to run on to school and he travelled to his office in Earls Court or his architectural practice in Cambridge, after which he brought work home or, for that matter, to his other home. For he maintained a parallel on-going relationship with his business partner, who resided in Woking, south of London. He oscillated between two abodes, two women, two different families (she had four children from her first marriage) and two groups of acquaintances. Besides these two constant relationships there were other affairs – which presumably kept him even busier and also, perhaps, kept his memories at bay.

What space in that frenzied, libidinal life was there for contemplation of the past? Would we, as children, have known or noticed it? Possibly not. He even had to arrange to take two sets of holidays. With us vacations were generally active periods, skiing in Austria, Switzerland or France or driving the *Routes Nationales* through France to Spain. I remember one evening at the small fishing village of Llansa near the Catalan-French border, he walked up a small hill above the port and then at dinner said to my mother that he had cried for the first time in years, thinking about his dead family. I do not think he noticed me listening. I recall being conscious for the first time of my father was a human being who could cry. Up to that point he had been a rock of physical strength in my eyes. I was six years old and I can remember wondering if his tears made him weaker or stronger.

26

RWANDA NOTES 2: FUNGI

Installed stained glass, Rwanda

The woodwork is completed. Battens of an African hardwood, copalwood or acajou with the consistency of supple oak suddenly "appeared". However, John the carpenter has disappeared. The Aegis exhibition team (led by Stephen and James Smith, who are creating the museum for the Rwandan government and people) lent me their electric saw and within a short time I was able to trim to size and fill all the routed grooves in the frame.

Most annoying... I cut myself, an unpleasant gash, two inches long diagonally down my right thumb. Washed with TCP and bandages to staunch the copious bleeding, it does not look as if it required sutures. I check my inoculation card. Fortunately I have a Tetanus jab. Should be OK.

Next morning: my hand has alarmingly swollen. James Smith is a surgeon. He found time in his overwhelmingly crowded schedule to come by.

"Did you disinfect it?"
"Yes, TCP."
"Tetanus?"
"Yes."
"Should be OK."

I must have some exterior iron balcony or railing made to protect the stained-glass windows from itinerant workers who touch or prod everything. The people I have met here seem to combine cool reserve, observation, and distance with a tactile fascination, closely personal. It would be a great pity if, after surviving the journey here, the stained glass were to be wrecked in situ. A blacksmith working on a gate says he will do this within two days. He understands my sketch for the railings, shows how he will make and fix them, clearly knows what he is talking about. He is delightful. Open, smiling.

"Two days?"

Is this more of the Rwandan vague optimism on all matters of time? "Tomorrow" is a typical answer to any question. When will the wall be completed? "Tomorrow" (a retaining wall around the whole compound). When will the car park be ready? (Intended to accommodate hundreds of cars and buses, and which is now an uneven dirt acreage). "Tomorrow". When will the plasterers finish? "Tomorrow."

There are about 700 people engaged on site at all stages of work, from those carrying raw materials, to plasterers, electricians, plumbers, carpenters, men tarring the concrete walls of the mass tombs (actual tombs where many of the dead, disinterred and discovered years after the genocide, have been given burial), bricklayers working with diminutive trowels the size of fish-knives until suddenly a consignment of trowels appears and work accelerates. There are painters, floor-tilers, carpenters, museum installation teams with completed graphics that have been flown-in in giant boxes, their texts in three languages, Kenya-Rwanda, French and English. It is all going on simultaneously. Dozens of people mill around, awaiting instructions. From the air it must look like one of those zany overpopulated cartoons of a building site at every stage of its evolution. Or an African version of *Where's Wally*. Work progresses three steps forwards, two steps back. Muddy bare feet leave their prints on the newly laid black carpets. Streams of women bear shallow baskets of earth and brick on their heads, proceeding in barefoot caravans, all day, slowly, to a rhythm that does not exist in Europe. And yet the blacksmith inspires me with optimism. Where will he get the iron? He seems to have the tools. I simply cannot install the windows before he has set up those protective iron railings.

Another member of the Aegis team sees my swelling hand and tells me to go and see a doctor at the Belgian Embassy, one who stayed behind in Rwanda during the genocide. In the afternoon I walk to her clinic. An attractive woman. She seems bemused or mildly irritated that a foreigner has been added to her list of locals to treat. She prescribes a strong antibiotic. There is only one pharmacy she can trust to give me the genuine medicine and she very kindly calls them to ascertain that they have it in stock. I'm in luck. On my way there my thumb begins to throb, my hand has inflated dramatically.

A woman, walking ten yards in front of me, carries a large flat wicker tray with huge parasol mushrooms on her head. From one angle it looks as if she is wearing the world's largest sombrero. Moving closer I see that the fungi resemble shield-shaped Entoloma which could easily be confused with Entolomo Lividum, which is poisonous, deadly. The mushrooms look sinister. Or is this evil impression caused by the woman's gait? She walks with a pronounced limp. An orthopaedic problem? Her hip or maybe her thigh? As I pass closer to her, better to view the mushrooms, I see that she has a long scar from her cheek to her shoulder. A machete must once have sliced through her ear, for it appears slightly disconnected, the cut parts healed but ill-matched.

My thumb is now throbbing, pulsing up my arm to my armpit and neck.

27

TIDAL

Over the last three decades of his life memory rose in my father, at first like a weekly tide and later flooding in two or three times daily. In the last decade it seemed as though the tide was always there, high-lapping his consciousness. And more than *The Ancient Mariner* he constantly externalized the events he survived, retold his story. The lost and the murdered. They lived with him, urged themselves on his waking hours and intruded on his sleep.

Unlike people we know who have lived and died normal lives and peaceful deaths, the murdered would not leave him be. And as the need to tell rose in him, his impatience, even his irritation with ordinary conversation became apparent. He could cut his interlocutor off mid-sentence. It was as though magma seethed from a shallow seam, a fissure just beneath the surface of his being, some aspect of his past must out: the Final Solution, the death camps, slave labour, Nazi German methods of killing, a detail, a story, a chapter from yet another historian he was reading about the Shoah. Nothing matched this in importance. He could not control the flow. It had a force of its own.

At other times the Shoah emerged as a sort of trump card in conversation, almost defying anyone to talk when the subject was raised. The audience (for at this point interlocutors became an audience) were cowed; they generally fell silent in polite deference or fascination. For the subject has its own magnetism and, besides that, my father became animated, urgent, his persona riveting when he spoke of the Shoah. His pale blue eyes were keen – how much sharper black pupils look in clear blue – and stared into his listeners' eyes, alert to the effect of his words. He seemed to draw strength as the listener visibly slumped as though internally pummelled by a succession of blows. Who would not? In his quiet compelling voice my father related appalling things.

He once told me, it must be over 20 years ago, that Jeffrey Archer lunched with him in a pub in Cambridge and questioned him for an hour about his experiences, on the edge of his seat. And when they were about to leave the Panton Arms to go their separate ways Archer said to my father: "I'd give anything to have been there, in Auschwitz."

One could never tell how deeply his words penetrated the listener's imagination. Was it my father's words or his eyes, the force of his persona that they would recall? One never knows at what point a person's mental defences lower like a portcullis down to screen and protect them. My father was keenly aware of the impact of his presence. He and his subject – the two were one.

One of Lucian Freud's patiently suffering sitters once related how the painter gained strength when he saw a sitter wilt at the end of a particularly long portrait session. As the sitter became cramped, exhausted by motionless hours of posing on a chair, bed or couch, energy would shift, like sand in a sand-timer from him or her to the painter. He would be charged by their diminished powers. I sometimes observed this sort of battle of endurance between my father and the film crew In Poland.

However, once he had had his say, if the camera team pressed more questions, the sand-timer would abruptly turn again, his blood sugar might drop abruptly and he became irritated, angry. They had outlasted him. All at once, he would be sapped of all energy. He either left the camera abruptly, energised, vital, almost striding off, despite the pain in his knees; or else he was outlasted, exhausted.

28

RWANDA NOTES 3: BLACK

It rained heavily last night. Today more bodies, skeletons with some sinew to them, were brought up to Gisozi. They have been discovered blocking drainage canals around the city. Ten years on from the genocide and its victims are still rising to the surface, disinterred by rain.

Small entourages bring in the dead, on draped stretchers or in coffins that are little more than makeshift simple boxes. (Where does the wood come from for these coffins? Is it imported from Congo?) These are solemnly lowered into the remaining unsealed mass tomb, observed by a few men as the drizzle slants at us. There are seven such tombs topped in polished black concrete terrazzo of which only one is still open to receive the dead.

The ground is too muddy for much work today. Only a third of the workers have turned up. There is no sign of the blacksmith. Blacksmith or black smith? All those words in English prefixed by black – blackguard, blackeye, blackjack, blackmail, blacklist, blackfellows (for Australian aborigines), black-leg, black market, black-balled; blackboard (at school I remember we used to call the white board that replaced the blackboard a *blackboard*, there wasn't a word for it yet). I also recall the first time I heard the term black applied to a brown-skinned man, I thought the adult must be colour-blind, the skin was so obviously the colour of warm burnt-umber. Had he never seen a colour chart?

There are so many kinds of black. Ask any painter. Do you mean Lamp Black, Mars Black, Cold Black, Ivory Black, (originally made from charred ivory – the name makes one consider the contrast between ivory and black, thereby making the black seem so much deeper and warmer) Perylene Black; or are you imagining a less than absolute black? – a Charcoal Gray, or even Payne's Gray? Or are you mixing black with Vandyke Brown in your mind? Or with a slightly redder shade, a deep Brown Madder? Old Holland manufactures a Vine Black – so appropriate – in winter, the gnarled snake limbs look the darkest marks in the Mediterranean landscape.

Or – "shouted till he was black in the face" – with the peculiar precision to *black in the face*, to *in*. Small touches of black perhaps in the mixture of the pigment; and also black in the face suggesting colour (more prejudice) discerned through the expression – there of course being ways, more often than not, to see the mind's construction in the face.

At any rate, this blacksmith certainly did not look at all black. In fact the pigment of his skin was closer to coffee, more the coffee one drinks, slightly *latte*, than coffee beans which are so dark as to appear almost a Sudanese black. Whereas the colour of the celebrated Rwandan coffee bean is itself not black but a warm deep Umber.

Apropos black, a man I know, the product of an English public school, an Oxbridge graduate, today a successful international businessman, active in the arts, in short, one capable of lucid discourse, was looking at my designs for the windows, or perhaps at photos of the actual windows, photographed, complete. In both windows skulls feature, at the base of steps, to their right in the first window and at the centre in the other. At any rate, we were looking at the screen of my computer. He saw the images, lit up on the computer screen – a fitting way to view stained glass if one is not seeing it *in situ* – and, seeing the designs, with the skulls at the base of each window, he said:

"But the skulls are white. I thought you said this was Rwanda? Oh no, of course…"

The comment slipped out, just like that. I looked at him, shocked, deeply shocked. He was confused by his own confusion and masked it with an ironic shrug. But he had not been joking.

The Aegis team are performing the impossible. It is starting to appear just possible that the memorial center and the exhibition will be ready for the opening in ten days' time. A few days ago it all seemed hopeless, everything was still in process including parts of the building, the landscaping, perimeter walls, car park, the visitor's centre, the main gates, electricity, ironwork. Yet nothing deters the fervour of the Aegis team. Faith that moves mountains is infectious. They are working around the clock. There is a sense of mission.

Hazy cloud and horizontal wispy smoke terrace the hilly suburbs of Kigali. This could be a landscape of richly verdant serenity but it is impossible to separate what I can see from what I know has taken place here. The lush green bananas and cane offer up thoughts of their harvest, of machetes.

One funeral group sat down on an incomplete wall for over an hour to rest. They had come to bury a body they had found, either that of a relative, or simply a body unearthed from the genocide a decade back, in one of the mass tombs. In silence, they now begin to snake their way back down the slippery mud track to the shanty suburb by the stream. They are a group, but they descend as individuals, a chain with gaps between the links. No one talks.

29

DRIVING TO CHODECZ

The start of our journey to Poland in May 2005 went smoothly enough. We flew to Berlin's Tegel Airport and drove round the city in two hired cars, Roman, Aloma and I in one, Mark and June in the other, and headed east on a mild sunny afternoon, crossing into Poland within an hour and a half. The *autobahn* narrowed to a two-lane route through forest with occasional tracks leading off on either side and peroxide-blonde hookers tempting the truck drivers off the straight and narrow on their return route east from prosperous Germany. Half an hour further on and the hookers were replaced by roadside stalls selling equally blond-tipped asparagus, plump, white, invitingly bunched in buckets on trestle tables.

On a stop before Poznan, we sat outside in a small restaurant on a town square watching the Corpus Christi parade to the adjacent church and ordered asparagus. Instead of fresh produce we were served a gelatinous bowl of powdered soup, wobbling and still powdery. It was a culinary taste of things to come.

We spent the first night in Poznan. Roman and Aloma each went early to bed and I walked with Mark and June around the 18th-century terraced town square, whose periphery, though not its centre, was unspoilt by modern buildings. Those edifices destroyed in the Second World War had been faithfully restored. The 16th-century town hall by Giovanni Battista di Quadro was fused with the church at the square's centre. They and the clock tower and all the surrounding buildings were dramatically lit and the cafes were full. From time to time riotous cheering rose quadraphonically from round the square – the source of some of the roars hidden by the centre buildings. Only as we had almost completed a circuit did we realise that everyone was watching the European Cup final. Liverpool had scraped back into the game from a three-nil, half-time deficit to A.C. Milan and now the game would be decided on penalties. Liverpool's winning goal was crowned with a quadraphonic roar from around the square that seemed to us also to fanfare Poland's proud membership in the EEC.

The following morning, May 28th, we headed east from Poznan in dry heat. Beyond Konin we turned off the arterial road onto a sliver of tarmac heading north between fields until we came to a signpost for Chodecz. We drove into a sleepy, little town. At first Roman did not recognize where we were and asked why we were slowing down. Had it changed so much or was the memory of it altered in his mind? He had returned in 1967 yet I suspect he may have been more conscious of the stir he and his companion's flashy MG sports car made on the local people than focusing on the place itself or the past. At the time he was forty. It was interesting to note that his 1967 visit did not seem to have adjusted his memory at all. Somehow it had not registered on his internal hard disk. On his return he related to us at home several anecdotes about that journey, in the main, however, confined to trivia reflecting the backward provinciality he encountered, such as how a waiter had put a British flag on the table. There was nothing spoken then about his past.

Now, on this visit, he did not mention that trip. Instead everything was compared to his childhood memories. Things were failing to tally with the images in his mind. He seemed to be seeing before him not the Chodecz of 1967, nor even of 1945 – when he had returned at the end of the war only to find that not a single member of his family had survived and that his home had been taken over by two other families and that the locals wanted him dead – but the Chodecz of 1933-1939, when he was aged between six and twelve.

Parts of the small town, like his father's sawmill, had been razed and replaced, but the centre was easily identifiable from pre-war postcards. Chodecz has a main square, a church, a few roads with most of the houses and shops strung out along them. There was the odd side street. It was a clean but dilapidated backwater. No investments into municipal buildings had been made during the communist era. There was no library.

30

ADJUSTMENTS

According to my father one church was missing. The German Evangelical church had been demolished by the locals, after the fall of communism. The townsfolk wanted no reminder of the strong *Volksdeutsche* presence in the area. The steeple of the remaining Catholic church looked different to my father. He declared that they had swagged up the lower sides of the spire with stone embellishments. He said that the original spire had been simple, with straight edges down to its square base. Authoritatively he explained that they must have used masonry from the other church in order to dress this one up. But when we looked at some pre-war photos Mark had got hold of, it was strange to see that the spire on the Catholic church had not changed at all. There were those same neo-Baroque scroll embellishments at the base of the spire, as detailed on the old postcard.

My father began to get his bearings. The first place we stopped was the school where he was filmed reminiscing. The school building resembled the children's drawings of the school from Theresienstadt but without its plane trees breaking up the facade – an imposing white structure on three floors, with a red tiled roof and white walls. Roman looked perplexed – was it different from way he remembered it? I, too, was puzzled. It was something to do with the scale of the school and its position in the town.

As a boy growing up in London, between the ages of six and ten I went to the University College Junior School in Hampstead. Generally, my father would drop me off by car near Kenwood House, a mile and a bit from the school. There was always a tail-back at The Spaniards Inn bottleneck where the road narrows between the 17th-century pub and the former toll-house. My father was usually in a rush to get to his office and so he let me off at Kenwood to run the last mile to Hampstead. Sometimes, when it was raining, I would complain. He told me on several occasions that when he was a boy he would have to walk *all the way* to school. He would describe the lake and the forest. He told me that there were some other boys who walked from even further than him but that neither they nor he complained. Some boys carried their shoes so as not to dirty them or wear them out and then they would put them on before entering the school. So I pictured my father as a boy wending his lonely way through forest trails to school. Polish waggoners passed the Jewish lad without giving him a lift. He accepted the exhausting distance as a fact of life. So did I.

Now, whilst he was being filmed in front of his school, I paced 30 metres from his school to the main street, turned right for 20 metres then left and then, finally, within two minutes had reached his home. There it was, number 21 Aleja Zwyciestwa – previously 2, Marshal Pilsudski. That was it. Two minutes!

It seemed extraordinary that such a discrepancy could exist between memory and reality. And then it struck me that this return journey was really dealing with two forms of memory. One was the pre-Shoah memory of his childhood, green and golden, like the world of Dylan Thomas in *Fern Hill* – a poem my father loved. That memory was a sort of prelapsarian construct. It amalgamated reality with the fabric of a child's mind, carried over and cherished along with positive memories of his family, the way he wanted to remember them, not starved, emaciated, dying, reduced. However grim some of the details of his childhood were, it was still a version of pastoral.

There had been family dissonance between a dominating father and the three eldest sons, each of whom he faulted for a different reason: with Shlamek, the eldest, for choosing a wife who was too short for my grandfather's taste and with stumpy ankles which he regarded as a sign of ill-breeding. He fell out with Peccio for his Zionist leanings, and then for his refusal to become the Torah scribe his father wanted him to be – he had fled from the arranged apprenticeship to a renowned *sofer*, preferring to work in industry, managing a factory; and then there was his choice of wife. As I mentioned earlier, my grandfather did not attend his wedding. And Peccio never brought his wife to visit Chodecz. Finally, Max rowed with Iccio, the intellectual son, for his embrace of communism.

Memories of these arguments and divisions, the ruinous arson of the family properties by the local Poles, my father's position as last in the pecking order at table and memories of always being slightly hungry, the residual sadness that hung over Max Halter's eldest children, Shlamek, Sala, Peccio, Iccio and Rozia, following the death of their mother, Max's first wife, in childbirth with the sixth child, lingered in the home. In spite of the energy and humour of his second wife Salome, mother to Zosia and my father – all these were recalled and recounted by my father as normal family life, with its trials and differences. They were good memories, of the beautiful lake, swimming, stolen fruit, the *shtetl* peopled by larger-than-life figures, the world of Jewish social and religious stricture in the midst of the Polish world of forbidden foods.

31

TWO PEOPLES

As far as the Jews were concerned, Chodecz was composed of two heterogeneous peoples who never truly met. The Jewish cosmos was separate from the non-Jewish. It was governed by Jewish dietary laws, codified in a different climate, annotated in a different era but observed by the Jewish community in the unlikely setting of the Polish countryside. So half of the town's population were surrounded by people who were encouraged by their clergy and centuries of tradition, to regard the other half of the town's population, the Jewish community, the Jewish race, as the killers of their Messiah. In actual fact there were other divisions besides the Jews and the Christians, the key one being between Poles and *Volksdeutsche*, each with their own church. The latter felt superior to the ethnic Poles. The former regarded the *Volksdeutsche* as outsiders, intruders.

My father's childhood oscillated between the physical reality of Polish rural life, his father's timber yards, the lake, forest and fields only a hundred metres from his home and, on the other side, the world of the *shtibl*, the *mikveh*, the *cheder*, the laws of *kashrut*, and the illuminated *Haggadot* which were the pride of his father's collection. Max Halter visited his second cousin, the venerated Gerrer Rabbi, once a year to consult him about major decisions of his life. Roman was never allowed to accompany his father. He was regarded as too unruly or inquisitive by his father to visit the great *rebbe*.

Side by side with the physical reality of Jewish life, the ritual slaughterer, the baker whose ovens cooked each family's pot of *cholents* for Shabbat, the synagogue and study room, there was the abstract world of Judaism, the spiritual dimension, fuelled by longing for another place, a return to the holy city of Jerusalem, repository of dreams and repeated in daily prayer. So father's childhood before 1939 was a cocktail of innocence and strangeness.

And then there was the other world, cold, sharp as a sudden bitter northern wind that swept in the moment the Germans invaded and conscripted the *Volksdeutsche* boys of Chodecz into Hitler youth, inducting them as killers in an accelerated course to the SS. Overnight it froze the sfumato dreams of childhood. The Gestapo arrived led by "the Oberst", the local SS chief – for whom my father was later put to work. Humiliation, confiscation, the laws of discrimination, continual danger, capricious brutality, sickness, starvation, and death. Death around the corner every minute, hour, day, night, week and month for six long years. In my father's memory that first world was chronologically and spatially haphazard but the second world, the one triggered the day the German Nazis invaded is accurate, to extraordinary detail, save for one part of his story.

Each moment was etched distinctly in his memory, because each day was a unit to survive rather than merely to live.

Ardyn Halter, The Way Forward. *Stained glass, Rwanda, 2004*

32

RWANDA NOTES 4: THE WINDOWS

Today the two windows are finally installed. The first, entitled *Descent to Genocide*, is recessed in an open room situated one-third of the way through the trefoil space of the main exhibition area. This first curved viewing space is about the process leading up to genocide: the incitement, mind-warping words poisoning the minds of children in schools broadcast on the radio, issuing from government. The message here is simple: words become deeds. Understand the truth of Heine's words: "Where books are burned, later they will burn people too." Then, between this section of the exhibition and the central one, whose theme is the genocide itself shown in short films, photographs, descriptions, in the local language, Kenya-Rwanda (large print) and then in French and English (smaller), between them is the recessed black room, black carpet, black carpeted steps leading up to the only source of light, the stained-glass window itself. The second window *The Way Forward* is in a similar recessed room located between the central genocide exhibition. It is the last section of the three, curving, clover-leaf shaped galleries and deals with the aftermath: the wrecked lives; destroyed families; the survivors; the permanently maimed; the rape victims, the women infected with AIDS; the trauma, the impact on society.

Like the first recessed room, the second has the same set of black steps leading up to the window and the step motif is part of the design of the window itself.

So there they are now, installed, both windows. My task is done. The windows survived the journey from Crouch End in London to Heathrow, from Heathrow to Brussels, Brussels to Nairobi, Nairobi to Kigali, from Kigali through Rwandan customs and the truck ride to Gisozi. They survived porterage up the muddy hillside to the site and not one pane of glass, not a single piece broke. Nothing short of miraculous. And now for the first time I can see them complete. While working on them, the light table only had space for three or four contiguous sections. Each section guided the next to ensure continuity of colour, so I worked by night to view them in consistent light.

When my father and I began work on *Yad LaYeled*, it was forty years after the genocide of one-and-a-half-million Jewish children, and that project was finally completed shortly before the time of the Rwandan genocide. In 2004 when the Rwandan Memorial was completed, reports began to come in of another genocide, or brutal ethnic cleansing in Darfur.

How appropriate is it to exhibit art alongside documentation, at least at this stage, now when the genocide was perpetrated a mere decade earlier? I wondered whether the organisers learnt from the steady evolution of commemorations of the Shoah? If anyone had, then surely it was the Smith brothers and Aegis Trust. A word about Dr Stephen Smith and Dr James Smith. They visited Yad VaShem in the 1980s like so many hundreds of thousands of others but, unlike them, they emerged stunned at seeing the documentary evidence of genocide detailed and they asked questions. How was it that in

England at that time there was no significant memorial to the victims of genocide? So, commencing with a couple of rooms seconded from the conference centre outside Nottingham – their family business – they set about creating *Beit Shalom* which grew to be the first museum of its kind in the United Kingdom. Shortly before it opened, they were invited by the Board of Deputies of Britain's Jews to explain, to detail what they were doing and their motivation for doing it. It seemed so implausible to The Board of Deputies of British Jews, the pillars of the British Jewish community, that anyone outside the Jewish community would spend time and personal resources on such a project.

I wondered how a Rwandan Tutsi or Hutu would react to the windows I designed and made. When perpetrator and victim can relate to art about genocide then, perhaps, this is a litmus of social progress. Could art be a measure of safe distance from genocide? Perhaps, I wondered, they'll simply ignore the windows until such a time as they may relate to them. Confronted with the terrible images of atrocity, the photographs, films of murder in process, the survivors, those remaindered, art seems to shrivel. I find myself wondering what right I had to interpret what these people went through. It is a murky area in which several elements reel and circle: the need to involve oneself; responsibility; the inappropriateness of art concerned with experience that is not directly your own – I mean that of your own eyes, your own flesh and blood. And then there is another aspect – geography. The lessons of the past.... is this a version of colonial reparation? These thoughts connect and yet swim about, not quite connecting. They will not resolve themselves. I cannot see a clear pattern to either my thoughts or my emotions. And sitting on the black, carpeted steps – a coarse thick bristly material – I felt the bathos, the hollowness I always do when a project has reached completion.

And I watched the Rwandan women walking past, carrying bricks in the baskets on their heads, two bricks at a time, towards the perimeter wall, flowing at a single speed, as though out of time, time as I know it.

Romain Rolland's words echoed in my mind: "Art can offer us consolation as individuals, but it is powerless against reality."

33

BLUE

The Rwandans are church-goers. Many were corralled into churches during the genocide (as Jews were into the wooden synagogues during the *Shoah*), and then grenades lobbed in, or the tinder wood churches simply set ablaze along with everyone who was inside. Last Sunday I looked in on a few churches and saw simple stained-glass, small windows in two of them. Perhaps the simple fact that my windows are stained glass alone will communicate to them, connected in the minds of Rwandans to the church life and a medium engaging respect, deference. Will the colours speak to them?

A friend in Israel, Amos Ben Maior, worked for over a decade in Africa. When he saw the stained-glass windows from photographs, he stared at me and seemed to recede into himself.

"How did you know," he asked me, "that death in Africa is blue?" I could not understand his question, nor had I heard any such anthropological explanation. I simply told him that blue seemed to me the appropriate dominant colour for these windows. It was something I could not rationalize. I asked him what he meant.

Amos said that, walking in 1993 in the crowded cloth market

outside the centre of Kigali, in a crowded semi-shantytown area a year before the outbreak of the hundred-day genocide in 1994, he saw a figure cloaked in blue cloth, looking at him. More than that, he felt the figure's eyes were looking through him. The face unsettled him. It seemed disconnected from those around him, though close to them. The face gripped him. It was swathed in blue, Amos repeated, the blue over his head like a thin cloak, a deep blue, rich, darker than Lapis, a mid-ultramarine. He quickly focused his camera, took the photo, capturing the image of the figure. Several times. Or so he thought. But when the film was developed on his return home and he eagerly looked through the prints, he saw the market, the throng of people, richly dressed women in their colourful cotton floral fabrics, the textiles with tessellations, brilliant against their glowing brown skins. But the man in blue was not there. He was in none of the photos. Puzzled, Amos methodically looked again, one by one, at all the photos. Between the two women in the gorgeous fabrics there was no one; he distinctly remembered they were shorter by a head than the man in blue. But he was not there. Amos could not explain this.

Amos Ben Maior is a rational man. Yet to Amos it is clear today. He is sure, certain that the figure he saw was Death. And he is equally sure, with the clarity of a man as comfortable with the world of facts as with the world of dreams, that the mid-ultramarine blue of the man's cloak and robe is the colour of death in Africa. He is certain that this was a vision of the death that was to happen.

34

CAN YOU EVER GO BACK?

During the three days we were in Chodecz Roman spoke his childhood world back into existence. Here was his aunt and uncle's store. They lived at the back of that tiny shop. To us it appeared as little more than a terraced hovel, with the shoddy rural Polish fibreglass-bitumen tile roof, so ubiquitous in post-war Eastern Europe. Back then in his childhood the shop had been whitewashed and capped with a neat thatch. His uncle sold the finest tea in Chodecz, wearing white gloves to dispense the leaves. After work, his uncle (wearing his other pair of white gloves) conducted the band of the local fire brigade. He also composed. His love was music but he could not live by it and after he married my great-aunt, he moved from Kolo to Chodecz to help with the shop.

My father introduced himself to local people. His face was positive and smiling, they took to him immediately, complimenting him on his Polish. Looking now at the photographs I took during the journey I see, as I felt then, that there was no rancour or bitterness in his tone or his expression. When asked by us whether he felt any resentment, he replied that the Poles had suffered doubly, once under the Nazis and again under communism. The same open geniality exuded from him when we visited the family home, a small two-storied building on Aleja Zwyciestwa, fronting the pavement. Its once white walls were now a dirty grey. The garden was about thirty metres wide and one could see how timber and coal supplies might have been stacked in the yard that extended back about a 130 metres to poplars where a steep escarpment led down to the lake.

The wooden frames and doors his father had made and the thick floorboards, snugly laid, were still in place, solidly true. Yet the whole house was degraded with shoddy paraphernalia and cheap furnishings. The only object of pride was the Audi that the residents' eldest son, a policeman, had parked in what had once been the stables at the back. The well at the rear of the house was coped with a tin cover. My father politely complimented the present owner on every tasteless decoration and home-improvement he had made in yellowing knotty pine with plastic corner strips at the joints. And so the tour went on, room by room, the owner proudly indicating his handiwork as though by each and every addition and alteration he pointed out, he thereby also strengthened his claim to the house.

Before our visit Roman, Aloma and I had discussed if we would ever wish to seek the return of family land and property, should Polish restitution to the Jews ever be offered. We agreed that none of us would wish to pursue this. So it was not with appraising eyes that we walked through the rooms of the house or the land leading to the woody escarpment over the lake. Yet the owners were nervous. They tried to assign policeman Piotr, their youngest son, to accompany us during our stay, to keep an eye on our activities and, I suppose, discern our intentions. He attached himself to our group for about an hour, seemed to get bored, and then disappeared. He reappeared twice on the two following days, keeping tabs on our movements. A year later, when my father returned with Fergal Keane to film *Roman's Journey*, the family would not permit them to enter. The same man, the father of the house, who had shown us around a year before, shouted at the film crew to go away.

In the family home, only the door-frames and floorboards evinced quality and craftsmanship. I visualized the grandfather I had never met, and have only ever seen in three photographs, selecting the cured planks and working with the carpenters or instructing them.

Inside the former Halter house

The visit to this tired and worn house, home of my grandparents, my uncles and aunts, where my cousins would have visited, none of whom I ever knew, seemed unreal. Yet, strangely, it was no more unreal than returning to a scene of my own past, one I lived through. It is the playground of St Michael's School in Highgate which I attended from the age of five until seven and of which I have clear memories. I went back not long ago, and I stood there before the neo-Gothic schoolhouse, hearing in my head the voices of classmates, Stephen Knight, Jeremy and Valentine Kirk, Barry Page, Nicholas, Henry, and Ricardo Yatim. I have only to open that door and the faces and voices are there. I can see the patterns of friends running along the avenue of trees or across the playground. My first teacher, Miss Sofer, the headmaster Mr Williams, hundreds of moments, the vegetable patch, sports days, my teachers' clothes, every song sung in music lessons, every word of them, all are there. The crafts lessons, short trousers, scraped and bruised knees, the field behind the school, the lavatories, and the sawdust scattered by the caretaker in the blue boiler-suit over sick on the playground. They are as clear to me as yesterday.

Once, round about the year 2000, leafing through a book, a local history in photographs of Highgate and Muswell Hill, of the kind that has since become so popular, I chanced on a photograph of the playground of St Michael's Primary School from 1961. Most of the photographs in the book date from late Victorian or Edwardian times showing two charming villages with quiet leafy lanes and roads free of traffic, well dressed ladies – a slower, more leisurely world. Suddenly I recognised my friend Nicholas, there on the playground of St. Michael's and, knock-kneed, besides him, back to the camera, about a head taller than Nicholas, unmistakably, I saw myself. The photo, one of the last in the book, is in black and white and it feels strange to be bound within the documented past when in my mind it is so vivid, not distant at all.

But you can never go back. Even less to a place you have never lived, one that consists in your imagination, a landscape, a village, a world belonging to a parent, peopled by faces from stories and a few photos or scrap postcards. And the passage of time causes us, however sharp our recollection, to see even our own experiences as disjointed from the present, sometimes so far outside ourselves that the experience could almost be vicarious.

35

CHODECZ

In Chodecz there was no sign of the Jewish life that had once been. Zero. The synagogue and *mikveh* (the ritual bath) had been burned to the ground in 1939. In 1939 about half of the population of Chodecz were Jewish. No memorial commemorated the former substantial presence of Jews living with the Polish population. For the proportion of Jews in Chodecz amounted to triple the national Polish average. Over 700 Jews from Chodecz had been murdered. So far as I knew from Roman, four had survived. My father and three sisters of one family, Henia, Nadzia, and Sala Pinczewski who all live in Australia.

Quite by chance, a few days before our departure for Poland, I received an email ordering a piece of Judaica from a Dr. Bella Freeman in Melbourne. Replying that I would be happy to send it, I asked her if it could await my return, since I was about to go to Poland with my father and sister, to visit my father's native village. "What village?" she wrote, in the convenient, informal telegraphy of email. Chodecz. Chodecz?! Her mother came from there too. Within two emails the connection to Chodecz was established. Bella is the daughter of Nadzia, the middle Pinczewski sister.

Then, just as our email correspondence was entering a rapid and excited flow, she suddenly became reserved, as though stepping back from her computer, suspicious of this extraordinary coincidence, surprised perhaps that another new person had emerged who shared the same source as her. I reminded her of the order of our correspondence and that it had been she and not me who had initiated it. Yet her suspicions had been aroused. And when I questioned her about this, she wrote that she felt uncomfortable, perhaps I was the sort of person who draws comfort from the sufferings of others. Nonplussed, I let the correspondence stop, besides which, I had to prepare for the journey.

However, a year later Dr. Bella and her husband came to visit my home and studios. It transpired that not only had her mother and sisters survived but one of her brothers too. So it had been five Jews, not just four, of the total Jewish population of over 700 from Chodecz, who emerged from the Shoah. My father was the only one to return there. The surviving Pinczewski family had settled in Melbourne and had sworn never to set foot again on Polish soil.

Roman remembered the sisters clearly. He said: "They always received straight 5's in their school reports and 5 was the top mark. I rarely got higher than 3's. My mother and father used to ask me why I couldn't be like the Pinczewski sisters."

When people in Chodecz asked Roman who he was, he told them he was a *zyd*, a Jew. There was quiet defiance in his voice as he caught them with his bright blue eyes. They looked at him. He did not seem like a Jew, but then most of them had never met one. A few asked him why he said he was a Jew. One of them said: "I am a Pole. And you now come from England. You are English. So why do you say that you are a *zyd*?"

As we walked through Chodecz it seemed only half-alive. The other half had gone, gone completely, save for the memories that remained in my father's mind. The place felt exhausted, drained of its life-blood. Chodecz never recovered from the double blows of Nazism and Stalinist communism. What remained was pallid, an anaemic shell. There are traces of charm and impoverished civic pride despite the shoddy roofs that replaced the former thatch, but the soul of the town seemed to be missing, replaced by a particular vacancy, a palpable absence. (I confess that the "soul" of Chodecz is only something I know from anecdotal memory, the memories told and retold by my father).

We could not find anyone living to remember the Jews. Had everyone over the age of seventy-five died? Could this have been due to the Polish diet, high in fat, vodka and beer?

Later in our trip we drove to the north Lodz branch of Tesco. At the time of our visit, in Western Europe when one entered a major supermarket the first things to meet the shopper's trolley were fruit, vegetables and flowers. Occasionally this was preceded by a news and magazine section. Here, in Poland, a vast avenue of beer and vodka met us: a swathe of bottles and cans five metres wide and forty long. It had its own inner checkpoint, presumably in case the shopper should set to and prove too far gone to dispense the required cash by the time he or she reached the main tills.

36

RECOGNITION AND ROZIA

When Odysseus returns to Ithaca, washed ashore, naked, alone after the wreck of his ship, he looks for a person to remember him from twenty years earlier, one whose lips would speak about Odysseus, the just master of the island, someone loyal to endorse his identity and connect the present man to the figure of the past. Odysseus meets Eumaeus, his former house manager, now degraded to a swineherd.

So too my father, followed by the film crew, camera in hand, sound boom at the ready, searched Chodecz, asking the locals if anyone was still living over the age of seventy-five. Mark the filmmaker was depending on a recognition scene. My father wanted, needed to encounter someone from there who could remember with him, confirm the past within his head, validate his memories.

Ironically, the one sibling my father heard about during the first two days we were in Chodecz was his sister Rosa or Rozia, as the family called her, the only member of his family to die before the outbreak of war. She died in an accident. We were outside the family home about to get in the car, when a fleshy woman with thick blond hair, like blown straw, wearing a white apron, rushed diagonally in a slightly deranged manner across the empty road towards us. With little introduction she launched into an excited monologue about how her mother had told her of the death of Rosa, my father's half-sister, who had been rowing on the lake in a small boat with two non-Jewish friends. The boat capsized and Rosa, who was the only one who could swim, dived down to try and save her classmates. They were about sixteen years old at the time. Both girls grabbed on to Rosa dragging her under to the weeds below. A bystander tried to save them. By the time he found the three girls and pulled them ashore, two were already dead. Rozia was hospitalized, unconscious. She died two weeks later.

Three deaths within a small community was a major event in prewar Poland. It shook the Jewish and non-Jewish communities, became a cautionary tale, imprinted on the memory of this neighbour when she was growing up. But after 1939 three deaths would have been inconsequential, mere details in the daily fare of atrocity. It was remarkable that this fact remained with the woman, whereas the fate of the rest of my father's family was entirely unknown to her. Nor did she seem interested enough to inquire about them. Equally intriguing was the conviction she held that we would be able to find Rosa's grave in the cemetery. And she pointed in the direction of the site of the destroyed German Evangelical church, north of the town. Roman knew that the Jews were buried on the other side of town. No Jew would have been buried by the Christian cemetery. The other two girls might be buried there, not Rosa.

37

THE MOUND

Before 1939, the Jewish cemetery had been separate, distant from the town. But now there was no sign of it. Instead, at the end of a row of new homes, there just was a mound of earth. The mound swelled to about five metres high where previously the land had been flat with a view to the wheat field beyond. The cemetery had been bulldozed completely and earth piled up. Elm and beech saplings had been planted over it.

Two men were working, plastering a house close by. Seeing us approach, their expressions brightened. They became helpful.

They confirmed that this site had been the Jewish cemetery. They kindly offered, in return for a monthly wage, to restore it, dig out the graves and, if we wanted, to maintain any memorial sign that we chose to set up to mark the spot. They had heard that in many places in Poland, Jews, Israelis, survivors or their families came back and some of the locals earned a secondary income from the job of sexton. They freely explained that they could use the extra income to help them to finish the house.

Did the Poles never wish to initiate any memorial to commemorate their former fellow townsfolk? Would it always be only the remnants of the dead who paid for the favour? Were these, the dead Jews of Chodecz, not citizens worthy of a cenotaph, a memorial? How many villages in France who lost half their population in the Great War or the Second World War let the event pass unmarked by a memorial?

On June 10th 1944 Oradour-sur-Glane in the Haute-Vienne region was destroyed by the Führer regiment of the 2nd Waffen SS Panzer division. Six hundred and forty-two men, women and children were massacred, some fifty citizens less than the Jews killed in Chodecz. Wikipedia states: "There was no universally accepted explanation for the massacre." The entire village has been left as it was after the massacre and in the graveyard there a striking memorial column naming all the victims. Was money to be the only incentive to commemorate the lives of the Jews of Poland? What of municipal conscience, or even pride? No, amend that to simple recognition of its citizens.

Yet, given the general indifference to, or ignorance of the fate of the town's Jews sixty years on, excused in part by the fact that the local people were only starting to recover from the legacy of fifty years of communism and they neither knew nor cared about the Jewish citizens who had once lived there, it seemed to me somehow fitting that there be no memorial, no sign. Nothing. This was nothing now. The landscape had been airbrushed free of the Jews. With the exception of Rosa whose remains were buried somewhere there in that extensive mound, all the others, the rest of the Halter family remains were scattered between Lodz, Chelmno, Auschwitz, the Warsaw ghetto and Treblinka. A void might be the most appropriate memorial, and that is what I also felt.

These words are very much counter to Jewish thought, which is scrupulous about commemoration. The calendar marked with Jahrzeits, *hazkarot*, the remembrance of progenitors. Memorial candles are lit in homes. Graves are scrupulously maintained. Following a death there are the seven days of mourning, the *shiva*, then on the *shloshim*, the 30th day, there is the *alyia le kever* – literally the "going up to the grave" as though both death and the act of memory are assumed to be an ascent, rather than a descent. The act and the thought of memory are morally considered to raise the person remembering.

For all my dislike of cemeteries, one could contend that this extended essay is in itself a form of commemoration. It has occupied me for much longer than any visit to a memorial or cenotaph. That word, cenotaph, originates in the Greek "kenos" meaning empty and "taphos" meaning tomb. This journey endorsed in my mind an impression of Poland as exactly that: a vast empty tomb for the Jewish people.

38

RWANDA NOTES 5: TELL THE WORLD

Stephen and James Smith have arranged a pre-opening event for the survivors and their families, two days before the Memorial Centre's official opening, which is to be attended by several heads of state.

Today a line of survivors, mostly Tutsis, dressed in their best, threaded in single file up the hillside. They waited patiently, many carrying furled umbrellas. They were quiet, each immersed in his or her thoughts and memories. Some had brought photos of the dead. (Just now, before I wrote "the dead", I wrote "the lost" which would mean also those missing. To survivors, of course, the dead are always the missing.) They, the Rwandan relatives, the survivors, give these photos to the documentation centre on a terrace above the main building. The staff there scan them and the relatives can place the copy in one of the alcoves where steel wires with crocodile clips display a rapidly increasing number of photos of the dead. Most visitors view these in silence, searching along the short lines with pegged images as though looking for laundry that went missing in a great wash. Some break into loud and uncontrollable grief. I saw a woman collapse on the black carpet in the hall of photographs in a fit of anguish. Her cries were terrible to hear. She was surrounded by a group of other survivors who stroked her convulsing body until the sounds she made stopped and her body writhed in silence until it rested, exhausted.

Stephen Smith thanked all the Rwandan people associated with the establishment of the centre, naming them individually, and then he thanked the Aegis Trust team who had worked round the clock and looked both elated and on the verge of collapse. And then all those others associated. When he mentioned me, he added that I live in Israel and that I am the son of a survivor of the German Nazi genocide. He went on to say how important it was to them that this, the first opening ceremony, was for the survivors, for the people of Rwanda. His tone was modest. His words were moving in their self-effacing simplicity. There was no applause. It would have been inappropriate. This was not a performance.

Someone told me, as I was moving to leave, that there were people waiting to talk to me. About ten, perhaps fifteen people stood waiting in a line. I wondered what this was about. Did they disapprove of the stained glass? Was something wrong?

The first to meet me under an awning set up for the opening ceremony were a couple. He was dressed in white with a white umbrella. She stood just behind his shoulder. I found some chairs on which we could sit. They looked levelly at me. I recognised the intensity of the look, like my father's gaze, one that streams into you, unsettling, needing to be heard, driven by a need to tell, to be understood.

Like the others behind them, in their turn, they spoke mostly in English, though some of the older ones addressed me in French.

"Only you can understand us and what we have gone through. Tell your people. Tell the people of Israel. For you understand us. Israelis will understand us. The Jewish people know. Promise to tell our story. Tell your people. Tell the world."

One by one or in couples, they said roughly the same thing. I listened to them and tried to reassure them that I would tell. Looking into their eyes I knew that however much I felt for them and with them, there was and always would be the chasm that separates those grieving from the listener who sympathises, the survivor from the person who is merely visiting. This is the gap that separates the survivor and the Second Generation, or perhaps it is still wider, even less bridgeable. The world can speak of this, teach it, strive to prevent it, but the human race seems partly programmed, perhaps genetically, to repeat it. Yet this does not mean we must stop teaching, stop seeking to prevent genocide, even if its lessons refuse to be learned.

I wanted to be able to tell these people something but mostly listened in silence. I thought of the words Camus gives Dr. Rieux in *La Peste*. He knows that although the plague is hopeless, all one can do is to try and battle it, against all odds. And as that thought flashed through my mind, I felt how inappropriate it was that I was recalling a work of literature whilst he was telling me of the actual disaster that befell him, the death of his children. As though sensing, knowing the distance between what he was saying and what I was hearing, one man placed his hand lightly on my wrist as he spoke and I could not move.

I tried to keep my word but I could not. A team from Aegis agreed to film me, reporting on the creation of the Genocide Memorial Centre in Hebrew, about the tenth anniversary, the on-going trauma, the need of the Rwandan people to be understood. The film was edited down to a twenty-minute documentary. It was due to be screened on Israel's Channel One and then, the night of the screening, there was a speech by Shimon Peres at a political rally that grabbed the air-time. Two weeks later it was again scheduled to be shown, but the anniversary memorial date had passed and so Sari Raz, who was then in charge of cultural programs, pared it down to ten minutes. But that too was not shown due to some other reason. When eventually it was broadcast, it was still further reduced to a five-minute piece, so inconsequential that it might as well never have been shown.

I thought of the quiet people waiting to talk and of their eyes, the eyes of survivors who know that words will never convey what they need to tell.

39

SOMEWHERE MY FATHER WAS MEANT TO GO

On the next day, Saturday, Aloma, who observes *Shabbat,* rested where we were staying at the campsite by the lake at Chodecz. We drove to Chelmno. My father had a general idea of where Chelmno was. But he had never visited it. He knew it was there that his mother Salomé, his half-sister Sara, her children (a boy and a girl, who were almost the same age as he, and of whom he was very fond), his cousins, and almost everyone he had known outside the *Metalabteilung* in Lodz had been transferred to be murdered. I think he did not want to know about Chelmno because that place represented a reality he had hitherto succeeded in avoiding.

It was where, according to the German scheme of things, in the late autumn of 1942, he was to have been gassed and buried in lime; then in 1943 or 1944, exhumed by the Nazis who, seeking to conceal their mass murder, cremated the bodies in piles and had the ash and remains thrown into the River Ner.

Yet my father escaped this agenda. Ordered by his mother in her last words to him, he escaped from the transport as it moved out of the Lodz Ghetto. Along with two others, he leapt off at a bend in the road by a plot of cabbages. The two others who escaped had hidden in an outhouse but were found and shot. He lay between the cabbages. His mother continued to her death in Chelmno. He returned to Lodz. Suddenly he found himself alone in the world. Not a single member of his once extensive family remained alive. He was not quite fifteen years old.

Writing this now, I can think of no systematic killing I have read of or seen documented as appalling as Chelmno. My mind has somehow blocked out elements read and heard, recorded in my memory, to protect my own sanity.

The smallness of the site and the vast scale of the killing there are scrupulously documented in a raw account by Shlamek Fajner, one of only two or three people to ever escape from Chelmno. It is a document so chilling that reading it one's flesh crawls. Chelmno was a funnel narrowing rapidly to a horrible death. Indeed the word funnel is very close to the specific word and idea the Germans had in mind when, in some camps, they created enclosed, camouflaged fences, herding pens called *Die Schleuse* – English: "sluice". Later these were perfected into *Der Schlauch* – English : "tube" or "hose", as employed in Treblinka. The difference between these two was that the former had no turns and people could react (though do nothing, but nevertheless they panicked), while in the latter there was a turn in the route. It delayed the panic and the screams and meant that the killing was managed more efficiently.

Chelmno, the first death camp, employed this turn because of the shape of the house. Its cellar served as a perfect tube, neither too short nor too long for its murderous task. It is hard to hold even a part of that place and what went on there in one's mind. It is also impossible to forget. I cannot. The knowledge does not accommodate itself in the mind. Perhaps it is also because it was my family who were murdered there. Yet it surely takes no great leap of the imagination for one to consider all the other people whose lives were processed into death there, in that place, as also one's family.

Before turning to part of the account of Shlamek Fajner let me describe to you what we saw there on that placid, hot late morning at the end of May 2005. And before this, consider a few sentences written by Virginia Woolf, from her book *A Room of One's Own*.

What is meant by "reality"? It would seem to be something very erratic, very undependable – now to be found in a dusty road, now in a scrap of newspaper in the street, now a daffodil in the sun. It lights up a group in a room and stamps some casual saying. It overwhelms one walking home beneath the stars and makes the silent world more real than the world of speech... Sometimes, too, it seems to dwell in shapes too far away for us to discern what their nature is. But whatever it touches, it fixes and makes permanent. This is what remains when the skin of the day has been cast into the hedge; that is what is left of past time and of our loves and hates. Now the writer, as I think, has the chance to live more than other people in the presence of this reality. It is his business to find it and collect it and communicate it to the rest of us. So at least I infer from reading *Lear* or *Emma* or *La recherche du temps perdu*. For the reading of these books seems to perform a curious couching operation on the senses; one sees more intensely afterwards; the world seems bare of its covering and given an intenser life.

We walked the grounds at Chelmno because there were grounds to walk. We walked there not to discover more. There was no more to find. We knew there was nothing to see beyond the grounds and what was exhibited in the small three-room "museum" and a store, byre and stables 150 yards on where there were small piles of objects, glasses, shoes. My father bought a book in English on Chelmno edited by Shmuel Krakowski of Yad Vashem. The following nights were sleepless as he read and reread it.

40

THE FIRST DEATH CAMP

This was the place we visited: a low hill overlooking the meandering river plain of the Ner or one of its tributaries. A wooded escarpment descends from the hill towards the river. Beyond it are fields and the occasional contained stretch of woodland or forest. One is offered a panorama west to gentle mounds of terminal moraine, low grassy knolls. Topping the escarpment is the whitest church you have ever seen. It is the stuff of visions, dreams. It looks as if it was completed yesterday and it has always appeared this way. Its roof is steep and well-tiled in copper bands. The line of its steeple is true. It is surrounded by trees through which one can glimpse the whiteness of the church's lower walls. There is a dip in the escarpment to the north of the church and beyond this small gulley the land rises to the second building on the gentle hillside. This is where your imagination should place a big house. Consider one now a little larger than the house you originally had in mind. In some descriptions it is called the *palac*, in others, a "castle". It is neither of these, just a large country house, constructed on a north-south axis. It is built of stone and the walls to the upper floors have been plastered white. When you arrive at the house there are six or seven steps leading up to the main entrance. To the left of these are twelve or perhaps fifteen steps descending to the stores, to the cellar. In fact there are two floors above the basement and the top floor must have commanded a fine view of the plain of the River Ner to the west and probably also of farmland to the east.

So the white church, symbolic of Christ's goodness, is over there, gleaming to the south and over here is the manor house. It is not hard to imagine the structure of this "palace" because in 1943 it was razed to the ground and the rubble removed. However, the lines of the foundations, twin-courses of well-laid brick, remain along with the stone-paved floor of the basement corridor. You can see where the steps led down. The storerooms of the cellar lead off from a main corridor running north-south. So walk your eyes down the steps and into the cellar. Once down you have to turn left and then sharply right into the main corridor. There are the storerooms to the left and more of them to the right. But these rooms are locked. The only way you can go is now forward twenty or thirty metres down that corridor to the end where a ramp leads up and out of the building. Beyond the ramp further north are two other buildings constructed by the Russians after the war. Standing by the ramp today, or indeed anywhere by the foundations of the building, one's mind easily and clearly grasps the simple reality of the German Nazi method. The ramp leads directly up and into a waiting bus. The bus has no windows or seats, only wooden slats on the floor screwed into supports that raise it off the base so that there is space for air beneath, or for hosing it down once it gets soiled. It is like the inside of a rectangular sardine tin. It could hold 40 or 50 people, but disencumbered of all possessions and clothing except their underwear 80 or 90 emaciated men, women and children can be squashed inside. The metal doors at the back can be hermetically sealed and locked tight. The journey to the forest is only about four kilometres. The driver has a lever. When he pulls it, gas is released from under the floorboards into the van. Appalling screams can be heard from outside. After ten or twenty minutes most of the noise subsides. The driver looks through a small glass window and checks that all the people in the van are dead. Sometimes, as chance would have it, the workers opening and unloading the corpses find someone still alive – easily despatched by the guard with a bullet or a blow.

There are eight, nine or ten such transports every day. The earliest transports to Chelmno were Gypsies – the Roma people, then Jews. When too many arrived, the church was employed as a convenient waiting space.

I saw the foundations and the ramp. After having read the passage written by Shlamek I can now no longer separate it from what I saw. He escaped to Warsaw, consumed by a desire to warn the Jewish communities about what was in store for them. There he set his testimony down on paper. It was placed in one of the five milk churns buried in the ghetto – The Ringelblum Archives, discovered after the end of the war. Shlamek Fajner detailed his own escape in simple language:

> On Monday, January 19, 1942, while we were being loaded into the bus, I let everybody in and got into the vehicle last. A few gendarmes were sitting in the front, but there were none in the back. On my right there was a small window which could be opened easily. When I opened it a stream of fresh air blew in. I got scared and closed the window quickly. But the others, especially Moniek Halter,[1] encouraged me to escape. I made up my mind and, whispering, asked my fellows to stand so that the stream of air did not blow in the direction of the guards. Then I opened the window quickly, put my legs out, slid down, grabbed the wall of the platform with one hand, and put my feet on the hinges of the back door. I told the others to close the window right after I jumped out. I fell to the ground and turned a few somersaults. I grazed my arm. I was hoping I would not break my leg. It would be better to break an arm than a leg, because the most important thing was to march forward and get to a Jewish settlement... All the time I called on God and my parents to help me save the Jewish nation.

Fajner was sought everywhere by the Gestapo. He was in possession of information, had been an eyewitness to events that they intended no one to ever know about. He was persuaded by the Jewish leadership to leave the Warsaw Ghetto. They helped him to escape. He had become too "hot" to have there.

It is thought that he was killed when the Zamosc camp was liquidated. There simply was nowhere for him to hide.

It is one thing to read the account and another to read it there, at that place and know what was done to 320,000 human beings, only 60 to 65 years ago. It is so simple that it is baffling. Virginia Woolf asks: "What is meant by 'reality'?"

It is quite impossible now for me to think of Chelmno, or hear the name without knowing in my mind what I saw there and have read about, even though it has now fused into something that is too broad to see or hold in my mind as an entity. It resists approach, yet it is there and my mind cannot deal with it.

As we later found out, this reality is almost unknown to most of the Poles living in the region, or indeed, most people anywhere.

41

READ THIS OR MOVE ON A FEW PAGES

The following is part of Shlamek Fajner's 17-page testimony:

Goldman from Klodawa, caught by the Germans, described precisely how Jews were led into the gas-vans. When they were led to the palace they were treated very kindly. An old German, about 60 years-old, with a long pipe in his mouth helped mothers get their children down from the truck. He even took infants in his arms so that mothers could get out of the vehicle more easily. He helped the elderly get to the palace. In a word, he moved the troubled people with his gentleness and courtesy. They were led into a warm room heated by two stoves. The floor was covered with a wooden grate, just like in the bathhouse. There the old German and an SS officer made a speech assuring the Jews that they would be taken to the Litzmannstadt Ghetto and would work there and become useful people. Women would manage households; children would go to school. However, they were told that before their departure, they would have to undergo disinfection. For this reason everyone had to undress and leave only their underwear on. The clothes would be steamed. All valuables and documents had to be wrapped into a handkerchief and given to the Germans for safekeeping. If someone had paper money hidden or sewn into their clothes they should definitely take them out; otherwise the money would burn in the stove. The people had to take a bath. The old German kindly asked everybody to go to the bathhouse and opened a door beyond which there was a flight of about 15-20 steps going down. It was cold downstairs, but the old German assured them that it would be warm further down the corridor. The corridor was quite long and led to a ramp, at the end of which a gas-van was waiting. At that moment the kindness ended. The victims were forced into the van with fierce brutality. The Jews realised that death was approaching and cried "*Shema Yisrael*" desperately....

On Tuesday, January 13th at seven o'clock, hardly had we finished our pre-death prayer after breakfast when the Germans loaded all of us, including Goldman, into the van. When we arrived at the graveyard, we started preparing for work; Goldman was told to lie down in the grave. He was shot dead. The first van came by eight in the morning. That day all the vans were extremely packed – 90 corpses in each. After the doors were unlocked, the corpses fell out by themselves. In spite of the fact that we worked extremely hard, unloading the van took longer than usual. That day the Jewish ghetto in Bugaj was annihilated. The vans arrived continually, one after another. From the fourth van, someone threw an infant out. It was still alive. The SS men burst out laughing, shot the baby with a submachine gun and threw the body into the grave. Throughout the day about 800 Jews from Bugaj were buried. In the extreme cold, we worked until six in the evening and buried nine full vans of victims. After work, five of the "pit-workers" were shot dead...

On Thursday, January 15th, we were again driven to work very early. We went to the graveyard by bus. Moniek Halter told me that the window of the bus opened easily with the use of a crank. The thought of escape occupied my mind all the time; I desperately wanted to get to all living Jews to inform them about the terror at Chelmno.

At eight we were by the trench. The first transport arrived at ten. Those were Jews from Izbica. By lunchtime we had completed four tightly filled vans. I should describe the whole atrocious process of searching corpses. Imagine such a scene: from a pile of victims one

German pulls a corpse in one direction and another one in an opposite direction. They check women's necks for jewellery – if there are some gold necklaces they pull them off at once. Rings are removed from their fingers. Gold teeth are removed from their mouths with the use of pincers. Then the corpse's legs are spread apart and a German puts his hand into the corpse's rectum. The same is done to women, but here the front part of the body is penetrated. Although the procedure was repeated every day, each time it causes us furious anger.

By dinner I heard sad news: my dear parents and brother were already lying in the grave. At one in the afternoon we went back to work. I was trying to get closer to the dead to look at my family for the last time. I was hit by the "warm hearted" German with a pipe and "the Whip" shot at me. He missed. I do not know if that was intentional. But I was still alive. Not paying attention to the pain, I worked very fast to forget about the terrible loss, at least for a moment. I was alone in this world. Of my whole family, which consisted of 60 people, I was the only one still alive. Before evening, while we were helping the gravediggers bury the corpses, I put my spade aside and together with Podchelbnik said the *Kaddish* quietly. Three "pit-workers" were shot dead before they left the grave.

The account by Shlamek of Iczbicya Kuyawska (where my father's cousins lived) in its precise detailing of the German atrocities was intended to awaken those Jews still clinging to false hopes. He left no space for ambiguity. It is now fixed in my mind and I doubt I will ever forget it. Perhaps I wish that I could. Should not such things carry a mental health warning and be placed, like poisonous substances, in the *Separanda* section of a pharmacy beyond the access of an individual? The immediate response that springs to mind is the argument that since we are all different, we each can bear different degrees of reality. To each his quantum of tolerance, on this subject or any other.

We endure pain to differing degrees, as we do knowledge of atrocity. Later on our journey, seeing the way in which visitors walked through Auschwitz-Birkenau, I observed people's different degrees of receptivity to the evidence of mass extermination, as in the past I have observed at The Ghetto Fighters' Museum, or at Yad VaShem. Since knowledge permeates into understanding through different filters, how can we ever gauge the long-term effect of such knowledge on a person whose mind opens to know about the nadir of human capability? I recall the Israeli poet Haim Guri's contention that he did not think the *Shoah* should be taught in schools. He considered its reality injurious to the human mind.

Only three people ever escaped or emerged alive from Chelmno, so effective was the process of deception enacted on the victims, so immediate their conveyance to death and ruthless the control of the few Jews who worked there. My father does not count as one of those three since he never reached Chelmno but escaped from the transport to Chelmno as it moved out of Lodz .

A week before first drafting these words (August 2006) I read in the newspaper: "Last Chelmno death camp survivor dies." Szymon Srebrnik was compelled to work (chained at the ankles) at Chelmno from 1941 till 1945. He was the only one to survive there for so long. When he arrived at Chelmno he was eleven years old. When the camp was liquidated, he and the other remaining Jews were shot and left for dead by the retreating Germans. The bullet entered his neck, exiting through his mouth and piercing his nose.

He managed to make his way to a Polish farmer who took pity on him, removed his shackles and cared for him before the Russian forces advanced. In the camp he was forced to extract gold teeth from the mouths of the dead before burying them. Two years later, he was compelled to disinter the bodies and work on their incineration and disposal in the River Ner. His video testimony at Yad Vashem, part of the main exhibition, is harrowing. I chanced to see it there for the first time, three days after I read of his death. He speaks in level tones of how he found his mother's handbag amongst the effects of the dead, and within it her small personal possessions. In the video recording, at times close up, his pale, pasty face contracts over his eyes and what we see, the pain within the man, is barely suggested by the moistness in the corner of his eye that he locates with a fleshy finger, hesitantly, as though mistrustful of its position, outside on the surface of his face.

One is conscious of the inadequacy of the human face when it comes to the expression of atrocity. The face cannot express fear, pain or horror on a comparative scale. Physiognomy is limited to expressing the normal parameters of experience.

Szymon Srebnik

In *The Post Office Girl* [Sort of Books 2008 p.138], Stefan Zweig writes:

> There's an inherent limit to the stress that any material can bear. Water has its boiling point, metals their melting points. The elements of the spirit behave in the same way. Happiness can reach a pitch so great that any further happiness can't be felt. Pain, despair, humiliation, disgust, and fear are no different. Once the vessel is full, the world can't add to it.

Szymon Srebnik was cursed to live out his life, the rest of his days, with the sight, the smell, the sensory memory of Chelmno within him, there, for all his hours, conscious or unconscious. There can never be any meaning to compensation, not for Szymon Srebnik, not for my father. Roman remembered Szymon Srebnik from Lodz. I asked him how he thought Srebnik survived for so long in Chelmno.

"Ah, it was his voice. He had a beautiful voice. The SS kept him to sing to them at the end of the day."

In Claude Lanzmann's film *Shoah* Srebrnik returns to Chelmno with Lanzmann and sitting in a flat-bottomed boat, sings the songs he had to sing to the SS.

A little white house...
Lingers in my memory
Of that little white house
I dream every night...

42

A CONTAINER

Let me step aside now, for a couple of pages, to describe a painting, Pieter Breughel's *The Triumph of Death* (1562, The Prado, Madrid), and how it has come to influence the way I think about Chelmno.

Within this single canvas (measuring 776 mm x 1089 mm) the deaths of hundreds of people are detailed and that of thousands of others suggested. The bare form of the landscape resembles several others by Breughel. A broad landscape of low hills extends to a seascape with promontories. There the similarity ends. Unlike his landscapes in Vienna's Kunsthistorische Museum and New York's Metropolitan, this landscape is almost totally denuded of vegetation. All has been ravaged by fire and war and it seems that the very earth has been undermined, as though moled from hell. The surface is caved and pitted, resembling a pie-crust, thin and hollow beneath. The earth offers no hope of rejuvenation. The land teems with the dead, the dying, the damned and those about to be killed.

This put me in mind of the Jewish myth that there are 613 seeds in every pomegranate corresponding to the number of *mitzvot* (commandments). On a number of occasions I attempted to count them to test the legend. It was so very easy to lose count – the colour, the nugget clusters, their glistening garnet beauty were distracting. Only once did I complete the count – 676 – and deduced that perhaps the legend was based on some wishful average, a pathetic fallacy, where nature conforms to religion.

Few paintings detail so many people. Yet, for all the crowding, there are also largely empty spaces. These are mostly on high ground, reserved for individual executions. Bodies are splayed on four raised pole-wheels, open to the sky. Carrion birds descend on the furthest of these. A man hangs by his neck, his head caught in the cleft of a branch, his body seemingly impossibly tractioned. Six figures wait their turn beneath a scaffold whilst Death is in the process of hanging a seventh. The six are ordered in a row, four and then two, their silhouette pin-heads outlined against the sea. They are unable to move, even though only one figure is conducting the hanging. Closer to the foreground to the right, Death is about to execute a kneeling man. Death's sword is raised high in the air. A man in red trousers falls from a cliff, backwards, his face to us. Then you notice that he is being pulled back by Death.

The movement of the painting is downward – towards valleys and lower ground – teeming with columns of people and skulls, armies, processions, untold numbers of people being herded away. It all amounts to a tremendous flow, like magma driven onwards.

Death is everywhere, individually and in serried armies behind Christian banners, bearing torches, sinking ships, tolling a giant bell. The rich tones of umber and sienna and ochre are offset by localised sepia, black, and the white of the shrouds of the dead and the togas of Death's officers. Distant towns burn and other fires blaze through the landscape, their smoke clouding the sky. In the background, armies do battle in a ravine from where there is no escape. A village is corralled by Death. Solitary figures are beheaded, hanged, dismembered, drowned, trampled under hoof. Death comes to a king, robbing him of life in his prime (he is dressed in his armour and his beard is black), gloatingly denuding him also of his wealth and power. Death takes the merchant and it takes the mother and child; Death slits the pilgrim's throat. Death catches a whole group in a net. Death takes the lovers, the gambler and the fool.

Cohorts of Death mass behind tall shields emblazoned with long crosses. They stand in their hundreds on either side of a long rectangular container of which one end is hinged open by a swing pulley whose centre pole suggests the full dimensions – for the other side of the container is out of the picture. Under the elevated door to the receptacle is another cross. On top is Death, beating two drums whilst another Death, mounted on a fleshless horse, drives terrified people within as he swings his scythe. The mounted skeleton is supported by a column of skeletons ready to flail the terrified crush of people. The cohorts of Death are irresistible. Individual skeletons in the lower right foreground drive and reap the injured and petrified people up a ramp into the container.

That box is unlike anything else in the iconography of hell in Western art. I am unable to see it without also seeing the photograph of the trucks used for gassing at Chelmno. It is about the same scale. The frenzy in Breughel's painting was strategically re-generated by the Nazi killers. Perhaps it is the frenzy of the last-minute rush as the benign placid German with the pipe who aided the women and children along through the cellar, turned vicious and whipped them up the ramp.

Generally, the German Nazis strenuously, systematically, avoided scenes of panic, using duplicity wherever possible to beguile their victims into still hoping that they were being led to life elsewhere – the natural refuge of sane minds who hoped and prayed for human logic.

The terror of those herded to their deaths in the painting is remarkably vivid. In Breughel the people are dressed. Unlike the German Nazis, death is not particularly interested in stripping them of their assets. Here, with the exception of the king and the merchant, the people are just stripped of their lives.

Common to Breughel's painting and the Nazi methods is the ruthless, unflinching thoroughness of the enterprise of death. It is relentless. Since visiting Chelmno I cannot see Breughel's great painting without thinking of the gas vans for transporting the living to their death. One inevitably recalls the other. This reaction is, of course, subjective. I cannot read Eliot's "A crowd flowed over London bridge, so many,/ I had not thought death had undone so many" without, as Eliot himself acknowledges, hearing the echo of Dante's vestibule of the futile which inspired his lines: "*e dietro le venia si lunga tratta/ di gente , ch'io non averei creduto/ che morte tanta n'avesse disfatta*" or without seeing the columns of the living being processed to death in my mind's eye.

It is hard to disengage poem or image from subsequent events, hard not to conclude that in some way the artist or poet have been prescient, have plumbed with their imagination the depths to which humankind will descend. For example, it is difficult not to feel that Franz Kafka foresaw the concentration camps in his story *In The Penal Colony*, or that Heinrich Heine predicted, anticipated – is too strong a word – *sensed* the possibility of the Shoah in his 1834 extended essay *Religion and Philosophy in Germany*. To us, today, imaginative precedent is next to impossible to disengage from what historically succeeded it. How we see and react to genocide is coloured by those words and those paintings. And so a photo of Chelmno recalls Breughel, and *The Triumph of Death* reminds me of Chelmno and how at Chelmno it was people, people with families who drove other people, like my grandmother Salome, aunt Sara, and her small children and some 300,000 like them into such containers to be gassed with the exhaust fumes of the very vehicles transporting them and how, later, when the gas experiments were completed, and IG Farben AG were ready, they switched from exhaust fumes to Zyklon B.

Mobile gas van from Chelmno

People did that over and over and over again, not Death-the-leveller, not a metaphor, not a divine agent – mere people.

43

AN AFTER-DINNER DINNER WITH FAMILY MOJTA

The evening of the day that we visited Chelmno, we were invited to the home of Bogumit "Bogdan" Mojta and his family, who live in the tiny hamlet of Huta Chodecka, about a mile outside of Chodecz on the route to Izbica Kujawska. Bogdan was two years younger than my father, two classes below him at school. Roman remembered how Bogdan and his father carted wagonloads of anthracite for my grandfather from the train station six kilometres outside of Chodecz to his store and saw mill.

On our way to Chelmno in the morning, driving by his house, my father suddenly remembered the place. He used to be sent out by his father to inform the different carters who occasionally worked for him that the train had arrived. Sometimes he would carry notes and, on rare occasions, also money tucked well in socks which were, at that time, not tubes but like long bandages swaddled in overlapping bands from the toes up to the shins. Bogdan remembered my father arriving one day at his home and described with gestures how my father produced money from within his sock bandage. The sum was probably small since Max, my grandfather, would not have entrusted his impish, inquisitive youngest son with any large amount. However, Bogdan remembered this as "a wad of money". In his memory, my father was the son of a wealthy man.

Today, when one compares the houses that belonged to the Jews with the original houses of the Polish peasants, it is evident that the former were only marginally better off. Such at least was the case in Chodecz. The Jews had a network of trade, which, together with their entrepreneurial skills, enabled them to keep their noses just above the mire. There was no great market economy to tap into. Business and trade were almost exclusively local. Only once did my grandfather secure a government tender to supply timber. And yet the Jews' wealth was as boundless as the peasant Poles' imagination.

To the Poles, the life of the Jews seemed a mystery and their customs incomprehensible. Most Jews dressed differently from the local Poles. Besides state education, they had their own religious school. They had their own ritual bath. They slaughtered their animals in a different way. Many Jews travelled to other towns or received visitors from beyond the district. They were busy, initiated trade – they had to because the rules were weighted against them. They paid rent to buy and clear forests and employed locals to work for them. They could just about afford to buy machinery – they knew that new technology gave them the edge. So here was the mystery: when the Jews departed taking with them to Lodz Ghetto only what they could carry, where did they secrete their wealth? This question troubled Bogdan and resurfaced time and again during the evening when his family hosted us.

Two tables had been joined together to form an impressive square covered by a crisply ironed white tablecloth in the large lower mezzanine floor of the farmhouse. Bogdan is a lean farmer with keen blue eyes, a lined, tanned, triangular face, aquiline nose. He seemed younger, more energetic than was suggested by his full head of white hair. With us at table were his son, a car and tractor mechanic, and his two grandsons. The eldest was planning to join his father as a mechanic on the farm and service farm machinery in the area. The youngest, aged eleven, had a disproportionately large head. He sat beside Bogdan's wife, a portly woman with a faint moustache beneath a snub nose. Grandmother and grandson shared a healthy appetite, chewing in rhythm as they quietly despatched prodigious quantities of beef, sausages, bread and poultry. Bogdan explained:

"His head is not quite right." Everyone in our group made sympathetic sounds. June Kent solicitously expressed the hope that he would feel better soon. The boy obviously felt fine, his wide jaws chewing steadily on a leg of chicken, the muscles on his taut temples working with concentrated effort.

Bogdan's daughter-in-law was in the kitchen and only emerged towards the end of the evening, as though by mistake, when she entered the dining room in her apron. An endless succession of dishes was produced which my father, Mark Hirsch and June Kent struggled to appreciate, having already dined two hours earlier, and having accepted the invitation to come over for a drink at face value. Aloma, who keeps to the laws of *Kashrut*, could eat little but the fruit. As a vegetarian there were a few things I could try. At the centre of the table was a cut glass bowl of fruit topped by a pineapple. They had given of their best. My father had brought a large crate of beer. Bogdan's son poured shots of vodka all round.

Roman and Bogdan

The scene was slow moving. My father and Bodgan talked and we waited for Roman to translate what he chose to. Mark Hirsch needed a translation to make sense of what he was filming. There was ample time to watch the faces of everyone round the enormous table. And when one has more time than needed to observe objects they can begin to move slightly, heightened in one's perception. Their presence seemed magnified. Gradually it felt as though the table at which we sat with each separate item, each glass, the sausages in their little shadows of grease on the glass plates, the fruit bowl with each piece of fruit, the crowning pineapple, as if they were all distinctly sharp, focused, clear, no one object more crisp than another, as in a Dutch still life and then, as if someone were playing with the focus, they all simultaneously shifted out of focus, as though the colours had bled, like paint strokes laid fresh onto a canvas coated with turpentine.

Bodgan focused intently on my father across a corner of the table. To whom did my father's house now belong? Had it been bought from him and for how much? When my father explained, it seemed inconceivable to Bogdan that a Jew would ever relinquish rights to his own property. Implicit in this was the conviction that a Jew would simply not act in this way – Jews were too clever, too sharp in business. Something did not add up. And what had become of the untold treasures the Jews of Poland once owned? Bogdan's eyes sparkled with interest. He scarcely touched his food but sipped frugally from a small glass of Slivovitz like a finch dipping to drink.

He told my father that it was common knowledge that there had been a train of fourteen wagons packed full of gold belonging to the Jews of Budapest, which headed for Switzerland. The train had been stopped in its tracks by the Nazis just short of the border. The Jews of Poland also had wealth. Where had it all gone? Bogdan reintroduced the issue of money, wealth, compensation relentlessly during the evening. He had an agenda. By the time this theme had returned a third time I quietly and capriciously suggested to my father that he tell Bogdan that he had been present once, at the *mikveh* as a boy, at a discussion between his father and the other Jews who also sat on the town council. He should intimate that he chanced to overhear them saying, but could not be sure that what he heard was correct, that the Jewish fortune was hidden somewhere deep under the town church.

Towards the end of the evening Bogdan's son asked us where we had been that day and where we were heading after Chodecz. Roman told them of our visit to Chelmno, half an hour's drive in a southwesterly direction. Chelmno? No, they had not heard of the place. Roman explained that it was to Chelmno that the Jews of the entire region had been transported to their deaths. He also described how at Chelmno, in the forest by the road before one approaches the massive Stalinist memorial, there is a large sign, a map and in the top right, north-eastern corner Chodecz is clearly marked. It is at the edge of the local catchment area, though of course most locals were brought there via Lodz. Historically, it is known that people were transported to their deaths in Chelmno from as far afield as Liechtenstein, Berlin and Danzig. It was the first death camp to use gas. They looked at each other dubiously. None of them had heard of the place. They were shaking their heads.

A few hundred metres from where we were sitting, my father had witnessed his school friends clubbed by the SS recruits, by his own former schoolmates. Schoolmate clubbing schoolmate. Bayonetted. And then shot. It was a stretch of scrub, sandy ground with bushes and the occasional silver birch. We had driven past it on several occasions but Roman could not bring himself to get out and walk to the low sand quarries before the lakeside escarpment.

Now we were seated in a home in a hamlet on the outskirts of Chodecz, a small town on the north-east corner of the Chelmno map. Yet our hosts knew nothing of that place, of the *palac* or of the precise fate of all the Jews from the town.

How can words describe a vacuum other than by the effect it has on objects or people? I tried to visualize it not as emptiness, as vacated space, as so often I do when I walk down a street editing out, consciously removing eyesores, McDonald's, hideous chainstores or buildings I mark as architectural unworthies in my personal schemata. This time a similar mind-game began. I found myself playing vacuums, only differently, in terms of colour. I imagined a map where the coloured areas were removed, corresponding to where people have been removed from life. The blank spots, regions, were those emptied of people, forced migrations, exterminations. What would the map of the world look like? How much of it would be unblemished?

Would it be like this tablecloth with large white spaces between islands of colour? Cotton cloth tracts between the pineapple, the cut glass vodka glasses, the sausages and the cheese, the beer losing focus, ebbing thinner, less substantial, emptying into white.

Jolted back to consciousness, I asked our hosts if there is a local television and radio station in Lodz. There was. Did this station have history programs? Yes, Bogdan and his son keenly followed them. They were interested in world history and current affairs. Were there ever programs commemorating the lives of the former Jewish population of the region? No. They did not say "Of course not" but it was implicit in the tone of reply.

Mark the filmmaker did not think to ask Bogdan and any members of his family if they might wish to come to join us and travel to Chelmno, hard as it might have been for my father to return there, even the next day, Sunday, and film their reactions. When I suggested it to them, they considered for a moment, balancing the idea against the pre-scripted film. One could see that this small excursus, a forty-minute drive away, did not really fit the pre-ordained plan. It was not to be. There were dots to be joined.

44

LENS REALITY

I became uncomfortably aware of a surrogate reality created by the presence of the cameras, conscious that what they recorded would create a substitute world. However, both my father and our host Bogdan were at ease before microphone and lens. They were enjoying themselves. For them the camera provided the intimate circumstance for two very different explorations. For my father, Bogdan was a human marker, a triangulation point in his pre-war memories, even though Bogdan was not particularly helpful in this, principally because his own agenda involved a fascination with money: the Jews' wealth had grown into a deep and fabulous root in his mind, a mystery he needed to solve. He sought exact historical answers to what seemed to him the almost occult movement of finance, of tangible gold, silver, rare objects. But the reality of what befell the Jewish people was less pressing. It offered no prospect or opportunity. He broached the idea that he might represent my father, help him reclaim his family property, perhaps working on a percentage basis. I do not know if he knew and held a grudge against the family now living in the former Halter house or if he did not know them and cared not if he succeeded and they were evicted. To reclaim property was basic stuff. It seemed quite illogical to him and not a little irritating that my father simply passed on to other subjects. None of us was interested.

Although they had never been childhood friends, merely acquaintances through Bogdan's occasional work for my grandfather, the process of their re-encounter suited them both. So when a year on from our visit, my father returned with Fergal Keane and Fred Scott to make a different film, my father and Bogdan met up before the camera as "old childhood friends". Indeed, a form of parallel reality had been constructed based mostly on the present and very little on the past.

Two animated elderly men were meeting, each visually striking, one with white hair and a tanned skin, the other bald and substantial; Bogdan with hawk's eyes, blue and searching, my father with blue eyes, clear as a stream, passionately engaged or so passionately engaged as to seem interested in something beyond his interlocutor. One was a character, a working man, sinewy; the other had presence, carried breadth, a frame suggesting former physical power. Each was confident in his domain. This is what is on film. And what occurred in their respective childhoods, the interaction that happened or did not happen is subsumed to a few moments caught on consecutive good angles: the approach of Bogdan, his face a wedge of wrinkled personality looking into the lens which we take to be my father's face. My father arrives, gets out of the car, smiling with genuine warmth. There is the greeting, an embrace. Each utters the other's name: "Roman"... "Bogdan". The two walk away from the camera talking in Polish, intimate friends. The voice-over provides continuity to a different scene by my father's family home where this time they do not let him in.

45

REALITY AND FRIENDSHIP

I felt perplexed. Aloma did too, she perhaps even more than me, at how easily a veneer of acquaintance can come to be represented as a solid foundation of friendship. Appearance of substance can so easily flesh into substance. Both Roman and Bogdan were willingly slipping into a part, enjoying being filmed. They recognized each other as survivors of history.

It was as though a thin fabric had been placed over an object and now it was only possible to observe that object through the hue of the cloth.

For *Roman's Journey* Aloma was sieving, like a prospector, seeking the most accurate and telling versions from the numerous drafts of my father's book to understand which details were most significant. Moreover, there were some gaps in his accounts that did not make complete sense. This journey was an opportunity to clarify such points, or try to discover things that Roman had, perhaps, hitherto found it impossible to write or to speak about. She wasn't making much progress. The alter-reality of the film offered him a refuge from her questions. He had this other thing to do, the film, and could not be troubled. He was on edge and spoke in short discharges of compressed ire, as though she were a cause of pain to him at a time when he was already suffering so much. It was as if once again he was back in the camps, with no family. Our presence there did not help. He was an orphan and wanted and accepted no support.

I recall, when I was about nine, him telling me one day: "We come into this world alone and we die alone. It's every man for himself." It was not quite clear to me at the time quite what he meant by this, because at other times his mantra was "Family, there is no one you can depend upon except family." I must have been about seven when I first heard those words from his lips. I was confused. The next day at school I wondered whether my friends could be depended upon. And I also wondered if my father had any real friends, and if he did not, then who were the people he met when he was not at work? Why invest time in them if could not rely on them? And did that also mean that they could not rely on him? And is friendship to be measured by reliability?

46

TWO LAKES

In Chodecz, the lake below the campsite where we stayed is three miles long and perhaps a quarter of a mile across, bending in the middle and surrounded by embankments thick with beech, birch and pine trees. In late May the days were hot and dry, the mornings and evenings cool. The green water, veiled with pollen, moved slowly north where it drained down a narrow stream to a marshy lower lake, clogged with reeds. The water of the upper lake was clean. A few anglers dotted the jetties.

The only other lake I always associate with my father is in England – Virginia Waters, not far from Windsor where he lived in 1947. In shape and scale they are similar. On Rosh HaShana and Yom Kippur, after a three and a half hour *shaharit* service which, to me as a child, seemed quite interminable, we would head west out of London. (We drove on Saturdays and on Jewish holidays). The vaulted neo-Byzantine synagogue of Upper Berkeley Street was reserved for the backbone of the community, the wealthier, established families, those who bought their seats for the year – even if they only went to synagogue on the High Holy Days. Our family attended the overflow services held either in Central Hall Westminster, a vast impersonal Methodist Church, or Friends' House near Euston, an equally featureless Quaker edifice. One of the key songs, *Avinu Malkeynu*, would be sung by an old cantor in painful slow-motion. He eked out each syllable in croaking angst, as though piety and atonement attended the pain of his singing. The song is actually a very beautiful melody crowned with two lines in which tone and tempo change in a form of summing up, a volte-face, like the final couplet to a sonnet. They gather the song and embrace the congregation with a sense of well-being.

But not that cantor. His dirge was interminable. It brought one beyond atonement, back to malicious thought. Let it be his last croak.

The service over, the release one felt was tremendous. We drove out of London, past the Heathrow airport perimeter road, round Slough reservoir, and through Egham's leafy suburbs to Windsor Great Park and the lake at Virginia Waters. In my childhood and teens it seemed completely normal. It is what we did on Rosh HaShana (taking a picnic with us then) or on Yom Kippur, fasting as we walked the five miles around the lake and woods. Sometimes, if the dry summer had ended and the ground was moist enough, we picked mushrooms.

Until our visit to Chodecz I never considered why we went to that serene lake, edged by woods and landscaped in the tradition of Capability Brown with rhododendron and azalea gardens, gazebos on hills commanding ranging prospects down to the water. Although bordered by the largest open green in England, part of which serves as the royal polo pitch, it was wilder then, time-settled, with giant elm trees bordering part of the lake, their roots carpeted with deep-cushions of moss.

Our walks there were our *mussaf*, the afternoon Rosh Hashana or Yom Kippur memorial service. Was this the one time in the year when my father walked the past, permitted it space? For back in the early 1960's he did not speak to us about his family. To him this may have been a more fitting observance than murmuring *kaddish* in a bland hall with a congregation of strangers.

Kaddish, the prayer over the dead, carries its own geography of mourning. Said everywhere, over the grave and away from the grave, its remembrance is extraterritorial, common to Jews the world over, central to the liturgy for all Jews since the Talmudic Gaonic period. It was, and still is, used to separate parts of the service. There was only one family member over whom my father had said *kaddish* during the Shoah: for his father, my grandfather Max, during the exceptionally cold winter of 1942 in the Lodz Ghetto. There is the *kaddish* prayer and there is a specific Mourner's Kaddish. I often wondered if I ought to participate in the Mourner's Kaddish. Can you mourn for people you have never met?

There, in Virginia Waters with the giant gunneras along the thin moss-banked streams leading down to the lake, the chestnuts trees, broad cedars, lofty sequoias and Washingtonias, were my father's thoughts more on the lost than the living? Did he walk on those days of fasting and introspection feeling pain at his huge loss? Guilt at his own survival? Or bewilderment?

Now the lake of Chodecz, the escarpment of trees and the town just above it, brought them back, the faces, his parents, grandparents, brothers Shlamek, Pesach, Izzak, sisters Sara, Rosa, Zosia, his nephews and nieces, cousins, school friends, his childhood world. And with the reflection of tall trees in the still waters, rippled only by the occasional perch or tench surfacing to gobble gadflies and mosquitoes, coots scuttering out of the reeds, and a few swans mirrored in the green water, the happy times and the pain of loss returned.

47

DUCK SHOOT

For my father, to swim meant to survive. Here is his account of the duck shoot from *Roman's Journey*. It took place in 1939 when he was compelled to function as a retriever for the SS chief in Chodecz. He was about twelve years-old at the time.

> "one day I was rounded up, together with three of my Jewish friends and taken to the lake. It transpired that we had been brought in to help with a duck shoot, in the capacity of dog retrievers. The man who had ordered us to be rounded up was the Oberst, Herr Oberst as the Germans called him, or Major.
>
> By now, this man was practically running the town and was also the chief training officer of the SS in our area. He, his wife and three children lived in the largest Jewish house in Chodecz which had been confiscated from a family who were related to us, the Czyzewskis. The house, office headquarters, sheds, stores and stables had all belonged to one of my father's cousins, a corn and grain merchant.
>
> We went to the lake. The Oberst had two guests with him, and his dog, Fritz. In among the reeds there were ducks. It had been a successful shoot. Instead of sending the dog each time to retrieve the catch, the Oberst shouted out that we should retrieve the prize.

Apart from the dog, I was the only one who could swim and I kept on volunteering to get it. So I swam out, got into the reeds, got hold of the duck by the wing with my teeth and somehow made my way back, stopping now and then to do a little backstroke with one hand and holding the duck on my chest with the other. That was a little easier for me and allowed me to breathe. Then, when I got to the bank I would put the duck down on the grass and Fritz would run back with it and place it at the Oberst's feet.

This worked out for a while. I swam naked as I was afraid to catch a cold by jumping into the October water with my clothes on and then walking around in wet trousers, shirt and sweater. So I stripped very quickly and performed my task. By the time I got back to the shooting party, I was practically dry and would quickly dress again. But on the third occasion one of the guests insisted that one of my friends go to catch it. They chose Szlamek, who had been hit in the eye on the heder playground with an arrow when he was seven and had only partial sight in that eye. He came up to the Oberst and said in Yiddish that he might not be able to find the duck because he was blind in one eye. The Oberst and his guests didn't quite understand the Yiddish so my two other friends tried to explain what Szlamek said. When they heard, the Germans roared with laughter. I knew that neither Szlamek nor the others could swim but it was too late. The Oberst said something to his guests and one guest got hold of Szlamek and told him to get the duck quickly. We could see that it lay partly on the reeds and partly on a clump of water lilies. But to get the duck meant swimming across clear water for some 50 yards. Szlamek began crying and pleading. Then the Oberst shouted '*Halt.*'

Szlamek stopped crying and stood rigid and to attention. By the end of September 1939, we Jewish people in Chodecz had learned that if we dared move when a German shouted '*Halt!*' we could expect to be shot.

'One of you get it!' he shouted.

I knew that none of my friends could swim, so I quickly started to strip, but the Oberst made me stand there naked. Szlamek stood rigid to one side. I stood naked next to the other two. They were still fully dressed and clinging to one another and pleading in Yiddish, 'We can't swim, we can't swim!'

The Oberst went up to his guests and spoke with them and they began to laugh together. Then he turned to me and motioned with his hand and pointed in the direction of the duck on the water lilies. Fritz followed me to the edge barking excitedly. I dived in, swam across a corner of the lake and then had to search amongst the water reeds and the lilies till I found the duck. Then I heard shots. I caught the duck, held it by my teeth and began swimming back. It was heavy, and the way I held it prevented me from breathing. I kept on adjusting it to make certain not to lose it; I was afraid that it would sink to the bottom of the lake. When I came to the edge, I saw Szlamek still fully dressed, drowning. He kept going under and coming up making horrible coughing noises.

The Oberst and his guests stood by the edge and shouted to me to swim towards them with the duck. I did as I was ordered, placed the duck on the shore. Then I asked if I might now help Szlamek to the edge. This part of the lake had no shallow end. I was told to get out and get dressed.

'You are almost as good as Fritz and we may need you again next week for another shoot,' said one of the guests.

They all laughed, Szlamek had no chance. He not only couldn't swim but he wore trousers tied just below the knee. They must have pulled him under when they filled with water.

I carried the ducks back. On the way we passed my other two friends who lay on the ground groaning and bleeding. The Oberst and his guests went past them. Fritz barked. I managed to whisper in Yiddish, 'I will come back to you.'

I returned as soon as I could with members of their families. The Oberst and his guests had told them that since they couldn't swim they might as well run back home. As they ran, they were shot, mainly in the bottom, back and legs. Their bodies were peppered with tiny plugs of lead. Szlamek drowned."[1]

48

NUMBERS IN WATER

The lake was about twenty-three degrees Celsius, warm enough for muscles to relax but sufficiently cool to be refreshing. Roman and Aloma, June and Mark would swim across its width and back. I set my course for a jetty about a kilometre-and-a-half away on the town side, taking the distant church spire as my marker, enjoying being alone. Yet in the cool water, stretching a long, smooth freestyle, I somehow couldn't gain that blessed disconnection that generally comes when I swim.

I wanted to get away from the others so as not to discuss anything, not to think about the Shoah for a while. Yet, now that I was well and truly on my own out in the middle of the lake, all I could think of was Chelmno and how sixty-three years earlier most Jews from this region were driven down those steps, through that cellar, up a ramp, into a truck and... It did not bear thinking about. Yet it gripped me and would not let go.

I counted to five strokes and then breathed deeply, bilaterally, noting my progress from breath to breath, along the lake, towards the distant jetty, the halfway point, lap end. Counting strokes, counting breaths, and swimming against a clock are habits from a childhood of competitive swimming that has run on into decades in a Masters (has-beens) swim team. It possibly seems absurd or strange, but counting is a way of maintaining length of stroke. And stroke-length is a key to style and body position in the water – connecting pulse, quantifying effort. Stroke, breath, pull – the rhythm is internal and external, both become one. It is not just exercise but an exercise in meditation. And then, just as the habit of pulls and breaths was doing what it generally does, disconnecting me from other thoughts, from everything except its own meditation in movement, the numbers came back.

Three hundred and twenty thousand people murdered just at that one place. Three, two, zero, zero, zero, zero. As numerals the number was no more manageable than in words.

Over my head-wave, as I breathed left, along the lakeside was a small white house, much the same in scale as the "museum" at Chelmno with its miserable collection of human artefacts, a perspex box of assorted buttons, another of spectacles, a few pendants, a Star of David, a small *menorah* and photos of the *Palac* – before 1943 when the Germans tore it down to efface all traces of what they did.

The water at the surface was caught by lowering sunlight. Flecked vegetation and loose weeds glowed on one side with a yellowish aura, ghastly and beautiful, they seemed to be enlarged to a different scale, like particles under a microscope.

The Chelmno museum had a photo of the second commander of the camp, Hauptsturmführer Hans Bothmann, a stern, lean man with high cheekbones and tightly shorn blond hair, his strong neck buttoned in the collar of the SS uniform. His previous appointment had been to run the German euthanasia program. When I looked at his photo on the wall I thought: this man does not look a beast. He just seems hard and slightly out of focus, although the photo was not.

My father was filmed in front of the photograph of Bothmann, whilst he read and translated a letter a victim had been forced to pen to her family back in the ghetto, telling them how well they were being treated, what good prospects were in store.

The weeds only reached the surface close to the jetties. Now there was no sun on the muddy lake and what I saw when I looked down, between breaths was mostly dark, colder than the surface.

Roman in Chelmno standing before photographs of
Hauptsturmführer Hans Bothmann and a motorized van
used for gassing people.

Three hundred and twenty thousand.... Periodically, human gatherings are filmed showing over a quarter of a million people. The TV lens can never get them all in. And if a helicopter or light plane films from overhead and the mass of humanity fits the screen, then the people are too small to see as individuals. You notice trees, buildings, perhaps a bus or a side road. Such numbers suit media technology as poorly as they suit our imaginations. Wimbledon Centre Court -10,000 or 15,000? Old Wembley Stadium: 70,000? And even then, the birds-eye lens up there in the floodlights misses those seated under the upper tiers.

Lying flat in the water, I am about two metres long. Now, assuming that people lying down are ten or fifteen centimetres longer than standing up, because of the drop-foot angle of their feet at rest, and allowing for a twenty centimetre gap between people, then if one averages the length of a person as two metres – do the sums -.... 320,000 times two metres makes 640,000 metres which is 640 kilometres. 640 kilometres. The distance from Berlin to Warsaw and half the way back. And this was just Chelmno, the first and far from the largest of the death camps. And now I have reached this mapped image in my mind it still does not help me. In thinking about genocide, it is almost impossible not to return to the cul-de-sac of statistics.

Any four of those people were my grandmother Salome, my aunt Sara and her children Henryk (aged 5 at his death) and Danuszia (aged four at hers). They were family because I had heard a few stories about them. The other 319,996 could just as easily have been my family.

Two metres per stroke, stroke by stroke in the cooling water, I returned to the distant jetty, climbed out, saw the shadows of the tall pines lengthening, Prussian green shadows across the darkening water, criss-crossing the stills and the ripples, and a small row-boat heading back from the neck of the lake. The others were walking back up the path between the beech trees towards the campsite. I watched the rowing boat and thought of one of the few surviving photos of Salome, the grandmother I know only from photographs. She is sitting in a canoe, smiling broadly. Probably on the other side of the lake near the jetty I had just swum to less than two kilometres away. It is the only photo of her in which she appears happy.

On our last morning in Chodecz, as we were about to depart for Lodz, Piotr, the son of the family who lived in my father's family home, came across to us in the square where we were resting in the shade under the lime trees and pollarded planes. He told Roman that there was a woman in Chodecz who might have been from his class, who was interested in meeting him.

Aloma and I did not go to that meeting. I am not sure why. Perhaps Roman wanted to go alone or Mark wanted to film him alone. I can't remember. But now, with their descriptions in my memory, I feel as though I was there.

Her own features were more conventionally Semitic than my father's. She escaped death because her mother, a Polish Catholic, possibly because she knew the child's father was Jewish, certainly aware that her daughter's features were a passport to deportation, had equipped her with a letter from the priest. In this way she avoided being rounded up on more than one occasion.

She had quickness in her eyes, and humour. She remembered my father's family and recalled how my father used to pull her pigtails at school. She was fond of him then and seemed to like what she saw now. When he told her that he planned to come back in the autumn with his wife and second daughter, she said, "Must you bring your wife?"

As they were parting, she said to my father, "Who knows, maybe my father was Jewish?"

All this is from hearsay. And yet I have a picture of her in my mind.

49

A HUNTING LODGE IN LODZ

From Chodecz we drove to Lodz, where we stayed in a reconstructed hunting lodge, the Villa Daria on the northern outskirts of town, a *Gothik* pile rebuilt in 1978. The proprietors had done well by communism and had done even better since its fall. Their garage housed four cars, including a Cadillac. There was one servant in the house and two groundsmen, closer to peasant serfs than employees in the western sense. The father of the house was in Cannes on their yacht. A chestnut mare was corralled in a corner of the garden, shaded by towering oaks. The estate was fenced in by iron palisades and fronted by three metre iron gates that opened by remote control from the reception. Two bars of the gates were chipped and bent but had evidently withstood the trial of a crowbar. For some reason the garden sported an artillery gun. Some thirty stuffed trophies crowded the walls of the lobby and staircase. Hermann Goering might have approved. The only thing that seemed missing was a photo of the Reichsmarschall beside an elk or bison.

The hotel rooms vied with each other in gloomy eccentricity. There were small steps up into my room and a hazardous split-level floor between bedroom and bathroom. The high, recessed windows offered little light – one had to climb into an alcove in order to gain a view of the shallow lake beyond the trees adjoining the property. The day was a scorcher and the park and lake were flooded with half the population of Lodz out bathing and picnicking in the sultry weather. Mark wished to film the street in the ghetto area where my father lived and where he worked in the *Metalabteilung*. But Roman was mentally exhausted by Chelmno and could not face the places where he had last seen his father living or again confront his parents' image in memory, reduced by starvation and illness. He stayed in the hotel and I remained with him, or near him. Aloma went with Mark and June. But Roman could not rest. He sat in the garden a few yards away from me and I saw that he often read and re-read the same paragraph or page from the book about Chelmno, as one does when the words simply do not percolate one's consciousness.

50

THE BARBER'S HANDS

Pardes Hanna is a small town in Israel on the coastal plain, roughly equidistant between Tel-Aviv and Haifa. The old barber's shop belonging to Yisrael Altman is sandwiched between Reis the greengrocer and Beit Shafir, a traditional Levantine store selling every kind of grain, bean, lentil, nut, dried fruit, herb, fresh ground coffee and carobs – all out of cardboard cylinders, sacks and boxes. The aroma of ground coffee reaches out onto the pavement. Archival photos show that in 1953 their facades were as they are now, tidy, simple, business-like, but worn. When I had more hair on my head I used to go to Yisrael once a week. So I must have been there about a hundred times before 1987. Until recently I still went, but only occasionally. And then only really out of loyalty, because of what he told me.

Barber's shop im Pardes Hanna

The barber's mirrors, their corners flaking mercury, run the length of the main wall from the slatted blinds of the front window to the draped corner at the back where he keeps his change of clothes by a formica-topped table with a wooden drawer that serves as his till. He drops coins into the drawer where they boom on thin ply. The seats have not changed for half-a century, nor have his tools. There is the same razor and leather strop. A clutch of small shaving brushes on the fissured Hebron marble top resembles a crop of miniature wheat-sheaves or posies. I labour these details because the sameness of going to the barber's is part of the comfort of the changeless ritual. Yisrael, regardless of what I asked for, always gave me something along the lines of a short-back-and-sides and few words in conversation. He never assailed one with opinions.

To the right as one enters are those three formica waiting chairs and a small table with dog-eared magazines facing the mirrors and the backs of the two massive barber's chairs. Hanging by the window, behind the hat-and-coat-stand is a small old transistor radio. And Yisrael, the barber, would be there and until recently was still there, wearing his pale blue or white short-sleeved working top, buttoned up the front. He looked dependable, with a freckled puffy face, maculated arms, and solid steady hands that dipped the combs into mild detergent, shook out the customer's bib, efficiently swept the last customer's hair from the floor into the corner. In a moment the place would be clean and reordered. He wore wooden clogs with rubber soles and white leather uppers. He moved quietly and you do not hear his steps, just the faint friction of his nylon working-smock as it brushes against the chair.

By 2009 Yisrael's head was albino white, sheet white. The blotches on his forearms and paling freckles on his face were the only clue to his former ginger appearance. In 1987, shortly after I began going to him, the white of his hair was still tinged with red. He would have the radio tuned to the classic FM station 91.3. In May of 1987 he was listening to the trial of John Demjanjuk, dubbed by the press as "the butcher of Treblinka". One could hear it if you passed his shop or went to Simcha's store. Most of the nation had been following the Demjanjuk trial on the radio; but as the proceedings ran on into weeks, popular interest waned as Yoram Sheftel, the defending lawyer, sowed confusion with his endless streams of witnesses.

According to the Yad VaShem summary:

> The trial began on February 16, 1987. Demjanjuk was charged with crimes against the Jewish people, crimes against humanity, war crimes, crimes against persecuted individuals, and murder. During the course of the trial, it was found that the Ukrainian Demjanjuk had been drafted into the Soviet army in 1940 and taken prisoner by the Germans in 1942. Soon, he volunteered for service at the Trawniki SS training camp, and several months later was posted in Treblinka, where he supervised the gas chamber operations. He was horribly brutal, forcing the victims into the chambers with whips, pipes, swords, knives, or guns. He served at Treblinka until September 1943, except for a short assignment at Sobibor. The defense claimed that the wrong man had been put on trial, that in fact, Demjanjuk was not "Ivan the Terrible" of Treblinka. In April 1988, the court found Demjanjuk guilty and sentenced him to death. However, the ruling was overturned by the Israeli Supreme Court, which accepted that there was serious doubt about Demjanjuk's identity. Demjanjuk was set free.[1]

It was now almost 100 days since the trial's dramatic opening and the sensationalism of the live broadcast of the trial had worn thin. There was no one else waiting for a haircut. I was the last customer before lunch.

"Do you think that Demjanjuk is guilty?" I asked Yisrael.

He paused a moment, turned down the radio, looked at his comb and answered quietly. "You would not forget the face of your tormentor. I know that. I was there."

"Where?"

"Auschwitz."

"And before Auschwitz?"

He stood still looking at me through the mirror, his scissors in his fingers, open, waiting.

"Lodz. In the ghetto."

"Lodz. But my father was also in Lodz ghetto and in Auschwitz. In Lodz he worked in the *Metalabteilung*, the metal workshop... armaments."

"So did I," said the barber. "I was the barber to the management. I cut their hair and shaved them."

"Did you cut Chimowicz's hair?" I asked.

Yisrael still did not reply. So I continued: "After his parents, his grandparents, brothers and sisters had all been killed, my father worked for Chimowicz. He was fifteen years old, and had to find work to survive. The director gave him a job as a *Läufer*, a runner in the factory. My father was taken on by Leon Chimowicz, and in return my father had to give Chimowicz half of his daily rations as well as cleaning Chimowicz's home each morning, before work."

"I remember him well," said Yisrael, his eyes looking aside, down towards the marble counter, as though seeing a man's face, perhaps the line of hair at his temple, or the shape of his chin. "Yes, both Leon and his brother, Alfred." He traced a line in the marble with his finger.

"What were they like?" I asked.

Yisrael did not answer. He put the scissors down on the marble top then straightened them beside the other two pairs of scissors, the serrated ones, the longer pair, now aligned like cutlery. He began to straighten the combs.

"But how did you survive?"

"Me...?" He seemed to come out of a reverie. "When we arrived there, at Auschwitz in 1943, we stood in line, waiting, standing there, waiting for Mengele's selection. Doctor Mengele... Yes?"

"Yes."

"When my turn came he said to me: 'You, what can you do?' I replied, 'I am a barber.'

'A barber? Show me your hands.'

I held out my hands. I don't know why, but they were steady, steadier than now, like a rock, like this."

He held out his hands, podgy, white, blotched with fading freckles, yet steady, solid and dependable.

Yisrael Altman, the barber

"I was fortunate. I could work in Auschwitz. I was barber to the SS, for him, for the officials."

I looked at his hands and at his wooden clogs, like at Auschwitz, but rubber soled and leather capped. The barber who trimmed the hair of Chimowicz who saved my father, the same barber trimmed the hair of Mengele and the Wehrmacht officers in Auschwitz –

possibly, on occasion, also of SS-Hauptsturmführer Rudolf Franz Höss, the commandant of Auschwitz.

He raised his long scissors and then replaced them exactly where they had been.

"I will never forgive Chimowicz. He could have saved my wife. He could have put her on our transport. But he listed her and she was sent to her death. When we met after liberation, he held out his hand to me. I did not take it. I spat and turned away. I will never forgive him."

He turned to his work surface, staring at it for a few seconds, touching the razor's mat black handle, then shifted his hand and chose the electric clippers to trim the back of my neck. He powdered it with talc, pumping the black balloon lightly before dusting my shoulders clean with the broad long-haired brush. Then he held the mirror up for me to see the military, clean, straight line of hair at the back, that I did not want, but he always gave.

51

LAPIDARY

The following afternoon was sultry and we drove to the Lodz Jewish cemetery. The map of this part of the city seemed almost deliberately misleading but we eventually found the entrance to the vast graveyard, arriving not long before closing time.

Due to recent extensive vandalism caused by rising anti-Semitism – in a land with a nugatory Jewish population – the cemetery gate was manned day and night. We had passed through the entrance room when Roman suddenly stopped, turned abruptly and announced that he would wait in the car. He left us to decide what to do. Since there was water and some refreshment in the car, we decided to go on into the cemetery.

Roman had visited here twenty-three years earlier. He was in Warsaw with a group from London, led by his friend and fellow survivor Rabbi Hugo Gryn and several other survivors who had been brought over to England from Theresienstadt in 1945. They are known as "The Boys"– historian Sir Martin Gilbert wrote an eponymous book about them. On that visit, when my father said that he would rise early and take a taxi to Lodz to try and find his father's grave, none of the survivors would come with him. Yet Arthur Hill, a man he scarcely knew, joined him as he was leaving the hotel at dawn, would not let him go alone. They did not succeed in discovering the grave but at least my father did not have to search for the place of his father's burial alone.

Lodz was the cemetery of many of the wealthiest Jews in Central or Eastern Europe. From 1890 to 1942 the textile magnates, industrialists, traders, pillars of the community, were buried here in mausolea whose grandeur blazons their wealth and social standing. The Poznansky family's mausoleum is so large that it even features in a thumbnail vignette together with the other key tourist sites on the border of the official city map. Here is extravagant real estate of the dead.

We walked the rows reading, when we could, the dull protocol of Jewish gravestone clichés. Talmudic scholars or those wishing to advertise their piety, and the patrons of *yeshivot* – Torah study seminaries – had images of books chiselled in bas-relief on their tombs. For a Cohen there were the split fingers of the *birkat Cohanim*, the priestly blessing. Most of the tombs had the Hebrew letters P.N. ("Here lies") – who needs to be told that? Or the acronym T.N.TZ.B.H (*Tihyeh nishmatcha zrura bitzror hachayim*, "May your soul be bound in the book of life"). Uninspired formulae.

Hundreds – what am I saying? – thousands of people travel each year to visit Jewish cemeteries. They are often guided by lecturers who teach history from the graves, so to speak. How dismal, how frustrating, that our tribute to most of those lives springs from the reflection of the grim encapsulating markers of decease rather than on the creativity of the lives lived. And here we were, doing just this, or something very like it.

The Lodz Jewish cemetery has some 160,000 graves. Granite, iron, marble, lead – their cost and promised permanence are belied by their condition. Entire rows had been smashed with sledgehammers. Others had subsided, assisted by tree roots, whether planted in memoriam or seeded by the wind. There were shrubs, weeds, the accreted soil and debris of more than half a century. Lichen and acid rain had rendered many inscriptions illegible.

In the harsh winter of 1941-1942, the gravediggers of Lodz's Jewish Burial Society would not expend an iota of effort helping to lift, wheel or carry a coffin that no one could pay for. They themselves were probably too starved for acts of altruism. When my father appealed to them to help bury his father, they saw there was nothing to be gained from the young man, so weak that he was practically a walking skeleton. My father had to lug the stretcher with his father's corpse wrapped only in his prayer shawl, all alone, lifting one end and turning it two metres, and then lifting the other side and pivoting that two metres and so progressing, length by length, two metres at a time. He was watched by his mother, whose ankles were swollen by starvation, and who was too weak to do more than watch.

No one would help my father dig the grave in the ice-hard ground. He had engraved a small metal plaque to mark the spot, in his break time at the metal factory. By the time he returned in 1982, it had probably rusted and disintegrated. The grave, wherever it was, remained unmarked.

Leaving the cemetery's inner walls, I saw an olive tree to the right of the main archway. Would it survive the frosts and snows? A modest sign beside it stated in Hebrew that it had been planted a month earlier by soldiers on an officers' training course from the Israel Defence Forces. They had cleared up a section of the cemetery. Whilst Aloma went to the car I found a bucket and watered the olive sapling, thinking how fast it would take root in Israel, in a light *hamra* soil, and how hard it would be for it to root here.

52

POOLS

My parents first met in a swimming pool, training for the 1950 Maccabiah Games, held every four years and open to Jewish athletes of every country. My mother competed (and starred) as a swimmer scooping a handful of gold medals; my father participated as a waterpolo player. Their daily morning swim in Park Road pool in London's Crouch End – open air in the 50-metre Lido in summer, indoors in winter – was a central ritual of their lives. The early morning aficionados are a sort of heterogeneous club, including firemen, lawyers, broadcasters, lecturers, art-historians, photographers – a cross-section of society whose lives sometimes interweave outside the pool too.

When my parents were unable to swim they were out of sorts.

The afternoon was drawing on. From the garden of the Villa Daria hunting lodge hotel in Lodz I watched the crowd paddling in the park's pond and picnicking on its banks. Should I take a swim there? It looked rather shallow.

Why had I not thought of my mother when we swam in the lake at Chodecz? I could come up with no simple answer. I watched the children and adults swimming, diving, running, eating in groups on the grass around the large pond through the trees and thought about my mother.

For my father, my mother never counted as a survivor. Underlying this was his conviction that what she experienced was not survival in the same sense as the concentration camp inmates. She was not *there*. Hungarian Jews were rounded up by Eichmann in 1944. So, from his point of view, this meant that they were spared almost five years. And then, Susie escaped. All her immediate family and most of her broader family survived – her aunts, uncles, cousins.

So, for Roman, my mother's wartime experiences were brief, even fortunate. But then I heard him and other survivors utter similar comparisons between Auschwitz and Buchenwald. "Buchenwald was like a holiday camp." Their glib bravura being nevertheless edged with grim knowledge of the difference.

While my father was generally specific in detail and recall, particularly concerning the Shoah, my mother was vague. Names and places emerged like islands in a mist. They were relegated for so long by instinct, habit, intentionally suppressed that some became permanently shelved.

Yet despite her vagueness, my mother knew her mind, her radar working well in all weathers. One sensed that imprecision or a strategic vagueness must have served her as an effective tactic at some point, grafting to become second nature.

There must once have been a reason for her sentences to begin two paragraphs down the logical thought process, their pronouns engaged without previous introduction. "He said that it could be done today." It was disorientating: Who was he? What was it? The subject was either withheld or had run its course internally, surfacing later like a spring far down the hillside. From the outset there was no chance of logical flow, only questions begged.

Was this the habit of one who had been made to hide, to feel guilty about her identity, one who outwardly deferred yet, at core, remained chary of authority, focused on what she wanted, her GPS coordinates fixed? And did such a habit induce my mother to hide, to raise a smoke screen, alerted by her long-range warning system and protect herself, even later, when there may have been no need to do so?

Visiting Budapest with her and Aviva, my younger sister, in 1974, she could not face going back to see her school, her fathers' stores, or even face entering her former home. The closest we came was to walk past it – Hegedüs Gyula Utca 34, on the corner of Csanady. But she led us on, compact in her purpose; we reached the building, the main door opened. I glimpsed a polished terrazzo floor, an iron lift with a sliding door and that was about it. A lady stepped out. The door shut with a solid sounding ker-lunk and that was it. As close as she would take us to that part of her past. My mother did not want to linger but led us to the Great Synagogue on Dohany Street where her Bat Mitzvah was celebrated in 1939. The neo-Byzantine synagogue was closed for renovations.

Outside the Dohany, a woman was trying to park her car. She was alarmingly unsuccessful and could not manage to reverse it into place; she seemed distraught, her mind clearly elsewhere. She had not actually hit any other cars or people yet, but it was a close thing. I offered to park it for her. She gave me the keys and unleashed a flow of gratitude. While I did this, Susie spoke to her and succeeded in calming her. This lady's distress seemed to empower my mother who was now in a better mood, and ready for the consolations of Budapest's conditorei of conditoreis, Café Gerbeaud, for a Dobos torte.

Our visit to Margit Island, to the Olympic swimming complex was for my mother the highlight of our trip. There we met her close friend and former team mate, Eva Szekely-Gyarmati, Olympic 200 metres breaststroke champion in 1952, the first woman to win an Olympic medal swimming butterfly, the ex-wife of Dezső "Szuta" Gyarmati, three-times Olympic waterpolo gold medallist and five-times Olympic finalist, perhaps the most celebrated player of all time. Eva was also the mother of Andrea Gyarmati, an Olympic silver and bronze medalist.

Susie said something to Eva and then told me to get in and swim a few lengths of the Olympic pool. It was like an audition. Eva watched me swim butterfly, backstroke and front-crawl and nodded from behind her large sunglasses (she had already then begun to lose her sight) whispering something to my mother. "Could be worth training" or "He needs a coach" (My mother had been my coach for many years) or "Not a chance. Does he like any other sports?" or "Leave him here and we could make something of him," or "Have you been back to Café Gerbeaud?"

This, for Susie was home. Definite article, *the* pool. Britain had no swimming complex that could compare with this one, even if for her every pool is also that pool and all pools mean freedom.

53

MEDALS

My mother's survival – what my father would probably prefer to call her escape – does she now remember so little because Roman's account never gave her space to relate it? Her story, as I know it, was the aggregate of snippets imparted over four decades. It can be summarized fairly briefly:

On March 19th 1944 her family was forced from their home and into the ghetto. Her father, Otto Nador, owned two ironmongery shops at the centre of Budapest. He frequented café society, the Austro-Hungarian version of an afternoon club, prided himself on his memory and was fond of reciting Hungarian poetry. He had received no higher education, was self-educated and had built his own business, helped in part by my grandmother's brother Bela. His origins were never mentioned by my mother's aunts and uncles and cousins because his father was not Jewish, but a Hungarian count who had seduced Otto's mother, an orthodox Jewish girl living in Köseg, a town on the border equidistant between Vienna and Budapest.

The name Nador means "count". It is unclear if Nador was the father's real name, or his title, or if the name was bestowed to ennoble the illegitimacy. Yet since Judaism is matrilineal and Otto's mother was Jewish, then according to *halacha* so was he. He married

Bertha Fischer, from an orthodox Jewish family and since his background was under a cloud, it must have meant, in those hidebound social circles, that my grandmother and, by inference, my mother and her sister, my aunt Judith, were also regarded as not quite up to scratch in their Jewish bona-fides. The opposite, in fact, of *yiches*, proud genealogy that enabled others to trace one's lineage back to the great rabbis of the past. All of which mattered not a jot to the Nazi Germans who traced back Jewish lineage two generations. So far as they were concerned, if one grandparent was Jewish then so was the grandchild.

Eichmann's program of concentration, extortion, deportation, and annihilation accelerated in the autumn of 1944. Many of my mother's cousins, aunts and uncles received *Schutzpässe* from Raoul Wallenberg, the legendary Swedish diplomat who risked his own life to save thousands of Jews.

The day came in late 1944, when Suzanna Margarit Nador and most of her Jewish school friends were gathered, counted, listed, recounted and then marched across the Danube. Those who were better off, like my mother, had suitcases carried by porters at the head of the column (the German methodology had calculated that people would be keen to follow their possessions). She carried a small linen bag which held money, food, her prized swimming medals and some clothes. It was cold winter and part of the Danube was frozen deep.

Flanked by German guards armed with rifles, the column was marched out of the city. Quite why, she is not sure, but my mother suddenly realised that they would never return from this march. She gave most of the few possessions in her bag – including her swimming medals – to a friend. This reduced its bulk. She asked the friend to carry them on for at least another kilometre and then discreetly to discard them. Although I asked her several times she never mentioned the name of the friend or schoolmate to whom she gave her possessions, nor the names of others in that column of youth force-marched, walking briskly out of Budapest, none of whom ever returned.

Her mind made up, she removed her yellow, star-of-David armband from the sleeve of her warm winter coat, dropping it in the snow. She moved to the edge of the column, shook her hair loose and, as they rounded a bend to the left, she walked steadily away. A light walk, off, away with every step, to the right into a side road. There was no shout, no shot. Susie opened the gate of a mansion – did she say mansion? I don't think she would have used that word.

Close against the high garden wall of the large house she changed from her trousers into a dress, folded her clothes from the march into her linen bag and headed back to the city, consciously crossing the Danube by the Erzsebet Bridge, two bridges downstream, away from St. Margaret's Island where she might easily have been recognised in the vicinity of the swimming pool. She had crossed the bridge and was feeling safer when she was stopped by SS guards who were forcing Jews out, along another axis route, away from the ghetto. Either then, or later, she saw Jews shot on the ice, falling into the water (my mother said that there were some who fell backwards before they were shot and swam under the freezing flow and escaped).

With her blonde hair and blue eyes, the SS asked her to stand where she was, stand so that they could exhibit her to some Jews being marched away, vaunting her as an example of an Aryan *Gretchen*, racially superior to them. She must have been terrified the Jewish people passing might recognize her. Gretchen was right in one respect. Her middle name is Margarit, her nickname Greta, Gretchen in German, my mother's mother tongue.

How long she stood there she cannot say. Did she ask them if she could go? If she did – and she must have – did she smile at them? Did they smile back? She could not return to the ghetto but realised she should get off the streets as soon as possible, but while outside she should stay on the pavement (Jews were not permitted to walk on the pavements) in case she would be recognised. So she hastened to the nearest tram (forbidden to Jews) and returned to the original family apartment building on Hegedüs Gyula Utca where the caretakers were family friends. Their son was sweet on her. They lived a floor below her family's original home. She feared that she would be seen by anyone descending the stairs or the lift for the family apartment and other flats in the building were now occupied by Nazi informers.

The caretakers downstairs took her in and were able to contact her parents in the Jewish ghetto. She went to live with former employees of her father, Otto. She learnt the Lord's Prayer and the Creed, false papers were found, and under the name of Margit Kolacko, a resident of Pécs, a town 150 kilometres to the south-west, a place my mother had never visited, she was given work in a packing factory half an hour's walk from where she stayed.

Sketchily she recalls the impression of Russian forces confronting the Germans across the Danube and then the Nazis' rushed retreat from the city on February 14th, so rapid that they did not have time to blow up the bridges as they had planned or complete the deportation of the remaining Jews from the ghetto to extermination camps. The Nazis gone, the danger now was of Soviet rape and pillage.

Unlike my father, my mother never dwelt on the past and rarely spoken of it, although at times she started typing biographical notes. She tended to reply to our questions in truncated sentences. "It is unpleasant... Why spoil the present and talk about it... before meals... or during meals... or after meals?"

Part of her instinct to survive and her subsequent pattern of living involved focusing on what mattered to her. Not so much concealing the past as getting on with the present. And telling? She felt no such inner compulsion. Her voice would fade, changes channels, shift elsewhere, unlike Roman's that was filled with urgency as he spoke. Susie's energy returned when she recalled how, in April of 1945, the national swimming coach Saroszy gathered together the survivors of the team and a dozen of them set to work cleaning out the swimming pool on St. Margaret Island.

By uncanny coincidence, just a month later in May, or perhaps June of 1945 my father, with a yoke and two buckets on his shoulders, began to dredge out and clean the swimming pool in Theresienstadt. He worked alone at first and then, a few days later, was assisted by others.

For both my parents swimming was an expression of liberty, of pleasure and vitality. It is symbolic not in the Jewish religious sense of a *mikveh*, but in recognition of something much simpler – a love of water, the physical pleasure of swimming, the sense of freedom and well-being. And each time they swam they reaffirmed this. A swim is always good. I have inherited this feeling.

Since early childhood I can remember the family home decked with my mother's cups and trophies (most of them silver cups which were stolen in their first burglary) and literally hundreds of medals (those not stolen in their fifth burglary) festooning the walls like decorations on a Russian general's chest. Open the front door and, if there was a north wind gusting across the dip of Crouch End from Alexandra Palace to the north, the house would tinkle. Those medals, mostly ghastly alloy confections hung on coloured nylon ribbon won in years of Masters swimming, were nothing like the fine plate-gold, silver and bronze castings of her youth – but perhaps they were displayed to compensate for those she parted with on that winter day in 1944 towards the trains that led to Auschwitz.

And then just as I completed writing this book, almost apropos of nothing, my mother said that Lili Erenyi took her medals from her on the march out from Budapest. "Lili Erenyi?" I was surprised. "You never mentioned her when I asked you."

"Oh yes, I am sure I did. What do you mean? Lilly Erenyi, she was our neighbour's daughter. She was about the same age as Juci." (My aunt, her sister, four years older than my mother) "They were marching us in geographical order, so I was walking beside those from the nearby houses and streets. I asked her to join me when I escaped, but she was afraid. So I gave her my medals to throw away, to drop in the snow."

54

GOING TO THE MOVIES

In 2011 I invited my mother to see the film *Watermark* at the Screen on the Hill in Belsize Park during the London Jewish Film Festival. It was about the swimmers, the ladies of *HaKoach Vienna*, the Jewish sports club, the leading sports club in 1930s Austria. The director, Yaron Zilberman, had succeeded in tracing five or six ladies in their late seventies and eighties, cultured, lucid, elegant women, one was a psychiatrist, another a doctor. Some of them were former national swimming champions. Several had refused to participate in the 1936 Olympics, even though they were rated medal prospects. Zilberman gathered these ladies from Holland, America, and Israel, uncovering documentation, photos, rare film footage of their past as he took them back to the pool where they had trained, competed and then, on film, the former team members swam one more time together.

Although this was Vienna, not Budapest, Susie felt the film was about her, her world, her youth, her friends. She was on the edge of her seat. The swimmer's life of the 1930s was unlike the professionalism of today, the endless kilometres of training, twice daily between taut wave-breaking lanes (not ropes with the occasional cork float), with goggles, palms-paddles, body-suits, pull-buoys, flippers, electronic touch-pad timing, or medical tests of muscle fibre, recovery rates, lactic acid counts. *HaKoach Vienna*, like my mother's club was altogether more easy-going, sociable, a culture of sport. And my mother's adopted motto from Juvenal's tenth satire – *mens sana in corpore sano* [a healthy mind in a healthy body] – is consonant with the cult of sport and the outdoors embraced in the 1920s and 1930s, which evolved into the mass displays of youth in Nazi propaganda. Outdoor gymnastics in white T-shirts. Parade-ground callisthenics. Yodelling troupes of youths a-wandering near and far with knapsacks on their backs. Before it was entirely kidnapped by the Nazis most of Europe was doing it, including Jewish youth movements. Sporting self-discipline was relatively easily converted into disciplined sport, earnest, subsumed under a larger purpose.

Watermark was the past, my mother's past, the life-style she loved, and it had style then, social respect. The word milieu seems appropriate, quite different from today. She nudged me: "It was just like that – just like that!"

For a long time, I used to think that my mother's sentimentality was underpinned by nostalgia. Now I see that her sentimentality was veined with grief.

Auschwitz fence

55

MEASURE FOR MEASURE

From Lodz we drove on to Krakow where we stayed for two days, before driving to Auschwitz-Birkenau and returning in the evening to wander the town centre and the Jewish quarter, which is more or less what most visitors do.

We were all getting tired. The journey followed its prescribed route, driven by the film schedule to which Aloma and I were adjuncts. This journey, this film, these days could have been different. Aloma also seemed to have a scenario in her mind of what might have been.

When I read the accounts by the Second Generation as they "return", I wonder at their energy, the tenacity of their purpose. For example, Daniel Mendelsohn in his book *The Lost: A Search for Six of the Six Million* – exhibits extraordinary staying power. The book alone is over 500 pages and in a minute font. He never seems to flag. Desensitized boredom or dull neutrality of mind is not permitted space. It would be an admission of... of what? Weakness? Irresponsibility? Inadequacy?

As though afraid that his travels back to Bolechow and scouring the length and breadth of half the globe to trace six members of his family will not be enough, will not be adequate or commensurate to the "task". (I cannot think of a satisfactory word to communicate the adequacy sought by one tracing his family back, who knows that however thorough his search the route will always lead, eventually, to a dead stop at a chasm).

Did he or Jonathan Safran Foer in *Everything is Illuminated*, or so many others who have tried going back, not feel exhaustion or emptiness? They beaver away for hundreds and hundreds of pages, every detail dutifully recorded, possessed, obsessed by a notion that every iota counts.

Mendelsohn even introduces a parallel theme from Genesis. He interweaves his search with Biblical exegesis seasoned with Rashi's commentaries. One senses the writer's apprehension that his journey, his search will never be adequate on its own, so something *more* must be injected to justify the obsessive way it can take over the writer. It is as though anything less than the on-going Biblical exegesis would belittle both the subject and the author's quest. Therefore the parallel text, The Text, – what text is more important than Genesis? – is intended to communicate scale and import. The author is telling us that his subject is not large but vast and warrants commensurate scale in his book. But it seemed to me to be a mechanism adopted by the writer to fortify him against the sense of hopelessness infusing the search, the bewildering fatigue, the final dissipating absence that the quest and all such quests inevitably come up against.

I identify with such fatigue.

Whatever route you take, the space-time continuum, the gap between what happened and what you seek, between the place you visit and its imprint on time, leads to a grey shore fused against a grey sky, vacancy divided from loss, from which one can only step back.

56

FATIGUE & FREMD

We were in Krakow, a tourist magnet in its own right and the base for trips to Auschwitz – a different tourism. It was only a week. My reserves were at a low ebb. Aloma was also drained. Roman looked pale and at less than half-steam. Mark and June were flagging but would not admit it. At breakfast June made herself bright, like a netball captain bravely fizzing around a dispirited team.

Preserving the Jewish quarter of Krakow had been integral to the Nazi intention to establish a second capital for the Third Reich in that city. Jews would then become an admissible object of interest, indulged as the subject of an ethnographic museum. What location more fitting than the city adjacent to the site of the elimination of the people to be commemorated. Cremated – commemorated.

Just as a camera, when it freezes frames, reveals reality in ways the naked eye cannot see, does not isolate, so too it was the German Reich's intent to present the anthropology of a lost people through photographs and ritual objects, out of context and behind glass. Isolated like objects of mystic beauty or deadly microbes, the Jews might then appear both fascinating and repellent, of anthropological interest. The Reich could then present Jews to the world, safely taxonomised, a mysterious thing of the past, remote in the unreality of the documented image. Museum vitrines, and framed photographs are the ideal medium for expressing this. Only then can such ethnicity be acknowledged, safely and surely refined by extinction.

The German word *fremd*, which originally meant "exotic, strange, unusual" under the Nazis had shifted in meaning, connoting the "undesirable" or "alien". Once the object it described was safely extinct, it could then be permitted to revert to its original sense.

Ardyn Halter, Fremd *(detail), oil on canvas, 1981*

The photos I took of my father at Auschwitz show him older than I had ever seen him, drained. However, this was due more to our visit to Chelmno two days previously. For by the time we reached Auschwitz, the impact of Chelmno and what he had read about it had struck deep. He had seen his mother and sister and her children and his cousins in his mind's eye at the site of their murder and he had faced the reality of a place he had heard of but never seen, one he had managed to avoid till then. During the war, by the time my father reached Auschwitz, he was alone in the world. The memory of Auschwitz is his own but it was not of his family. For my father, Auschwitz was about his own personal survival. And as such, strangely, it was simpler for him to deal with. He had no one to care about but himself.

57

A WALK IN AUSCHWITZ-BIRKENAU

So divorced from normal life, the shock of Auschwitz-Birkenau is different to the shock of Chelmno with its white church in the trees, the account of the charming old German with the pipe assisting the children into the gas van for the drive along the rural road to the forest. In Auschwitz, like my father, I found myself thinking of Chelmno where Zyklon B gas was used for the first time on humans, including our family.

In Auschwitz, close to the site of Gas Chamber Number 4 (I think it was number four) and the adjacent crematorium are sunken ash pits, where some of the human remains were deposited. These small recesses in the ground were filled with water a vivid pea-green colour. Frogs warming themselves on the gentle banks of these ponds hopped into the green slimy surface as one walked around the edge, dipping underwater without making a ripple, and out of sight.

My father spoke to the camera, detailing the sequence of his arrival at Birkenau, the unloading, the selection process, the distance between guards armed with submachine guns and Jewish people, a ditch dividing them. With his finger, he pointed to where there had been guards in the towers by the fence separating the tracks and selection area from the camp on either side. He described to us how Chimowicz the Jewish manager of the metal factory from Lodz saved their group from certain death. He had a letter from Hans Bibof, the former head of the Lodz Ghetto, endorsed by Albert Speer, Hitler's architect and munitions minister. After trying to present the letter to the SS officer at the selection ramp, and after being struck to the ground twice, he stood up a third time and, his head bleeding, repeated in a steady loud voice that he had a group of skilled metal workers and he waved the letter in his hand.

Dr. Mengele, intrigued, came over, gesturing to the SS guard to leave Chimowicz. So the entire group of metal workers, men and women (and even their children) were assigned for work rather than channelled for immediate extermination – the only case of children arriving at Auschwitz and not being separated from their parents and consigned directly to the gas chambers and crematoria. Roman recalled many more details as though verbally checking what was before us against sharply defined photographs stored in his mind.

We walked a few hundred metres and entered one of the barracks. Within it was a group of men from the Spanish Basque region. My father described to them and also to us what it was like living here. He needed to talk and he needed to tell and it was easier to speak to fresh eyes and ears. He pointed to the three-tiered bunk beds, where two men had been assigned to each narrow bed, and then explained that in the Stutthof labour camp up by the Baltic Sea (where he and the metal workers were sent from Birkenau) the bunks were two-thirds the width of these. In Stutthof, 200 of the group of 700 slave labourers were worked to their deaths within eight weeks of arrival.

Auschwitz is a UNESCO World Heritage site with a visitor centre. I walked up the steps of the gatehouse, now the offices, probably the offices for the site then as well. Up on the top floor of the arched brick entrance where no Jew would have entered I looked down on the rail lines that led in.

Ronald Brooks Kitaj (1932-2007) features this very gateway in the upper left of his painting *If Not, Not*. Its presence assumes some understanding, some tacit knowledge. But what understanding would that be? The gateway is inserted into his painting (or the large tapestry of it at the British Library) directly, emblematically. It is not placed there to illustrate the opacity of symbols, how they presume to represent a subject but in fact do not. For symbols claim to represent a distillation, the essence. Whereas in reality they do the very opposite and effect a shift towards vagueness, and emotional stock responses.

R.B. Kitaj, If Not, Not

The presence of such symbols, like Kitaj's use of the gatehouse, can work unfortunately as a form of bona fide, a badge of serious purpose, making certain (actually uncertain) serious claims to represent more than merely the image of that gatehouse. We see it and assume a hinterland – of what? What tacit understanding is there?

One might argue: Could it be otherwise? Are there ways to depict this gateway, to communicate in painting what it means to come here as a visitor, to come and not necessarily to understand but merely to know something, a little of what happened? Can it be painted without the presumption of shared knowledge? How might Kitaj have achieved that without laying himself open to a charge of consciously or unconsciously manipulating the image? Well, let's go with this a little. Kitaj might, for example, have shown himself standing before the gateway, or could have conveyed in some way that the place had been visited by the artist, or seen in a book (for example a self-portrait where the image appears open at a page, viewed by the artist), or as an image on a wall of an interior. Any of these devices, anything but presenting it directly as though from the eyes, from the memory of one who was shunted under that gate intended for extermination.

Kitaj or I, and almost all of us, approach that gate as visitors who can enter and walk up the steps to talk to a brisk young lady, an official guide working in the office on the second floor above that notorious railway gateway. The official tells me that almost 500,000 visitors from many countries have already visited Auschwitz this year alone, the 60th anniversary of the end of the war and the fall of the German Reich.

She has gone off to bring me some brochures that have run out at the desk.

Now, I can imagine my friend David Cohen, who is writing a book on Kitaj, saying to me from New York: "Don't the palm trees, the reclining figures elsewhere in Kitaj's painting do this? Aren't they the equivalent of visual parentheses that say: "Yes, I am painting this in London or Venice CA conscious that the gateway to Auschwitz-Birkenau resides as a symbol in my consciousness, in a corner of my mind. And when I see the Birkenau gateway or draw it, I am also saying 'Such a fate was intended for me as well.' As in the Haggadah: each generation should see itself as though it has emerged out of the land of Egypt, out of the house of bondage, into freedom." So isn't this what Kitaj is doing here?

My reply: "Can this be done without also making larger claims, without shrinking that image into a motif? If only R.B.Kitaj had found a way consciously to express exactly this, had depicted the Birkenau gatehouse precisely as an example of the way genocide is made manageable, somehow conveniently shrunk when employed as a motif, a symbol used. Had he done so, then the gateway as motif would lay claim to a different understanding, not the understanding of the survivor, but the understanding that for Kitaj or for you or for me this could only ever be an image that suggests something.

Something not understood. Only partially grasped. For without the parentheses of self-doubt the direct image makes claims that are not the artist's to make (however well-intentioned he may have been). Kitaj's painting presents that gateway without the visual parentheses that would convey a degree of modesty, humility, regarding what Ulrich Baer called 'the illusory certainty that what is seen is what can be known.' I am troubled by art or literature on the Shoah that is itself not troubled by its own endeavour."

"Ahh. You are being too subtle by far," I imagine David replying. "A visual symbol is a visual symbol."

"What about Holbein's skull? The emblem of death strikes obliquely across the face of *Les Ambassadeurs*. Its presence is not blandly symbolic. There are endless ways to employ a symbol…"

But before my internal discussion gives David Cohen a chance to reply, the efficient young lady with the tidy golden hair gathered in a pony-tail returns with some leaflets. Although in a hurry, she glances at me attentively.

A little rudely, I pepper her with personal questions: "What is it like working here? How did you come to work here? Did you apply for this position or were you assigned to this place? Do you sometimes feel your heart leaden, oppressed, by the end of the day? Do you live in Krakow or in Oswiecim, the adjacent town? And did you grow up here? Were your parents, no, grandparents, here, back then? Is this where you see yourself working a decade from now? Can you separate the history of this place from your life? I mean do you carry it about with you? When you go out with friends, do you ever talk about things that happen to you during the day, at work?"

I could see her telling her husband or boyfriend or girlfriend or friends at the pub: "There was this nosy person today, asking all sorts of personal questions. The usual. We get them from time to time. I just ignore them."

Of course, I actually said nothing. I did thank her for the leaflets.

58

OTHER VISITORS

Roman went back to the car. Aloma and I walked on to the end of the camp. As we passed other groups of visitors, she asked them where they had come from. There were many Polish school children, much too young to be brought to this place. In Israel, children under the age of fourteen are advised not to enter Yad VaShem or The Ghetto Fighters' Museum.

There were English people, Americans and Scandinavians. Most were not Jewish. We met several groups of Italians and others, individuals not in guided groups. A Frenchman I spoke to said simply that he was in the area and that he had to come.

One group walked past us staring ahead of them at the path, their heads tilted downwards. They were mostly in their forties and fifties. My sister asked them where they had come from.

"Germany," the woman responded in a dull voice.

As Günter Grass has written: "History for the German people is like a sewer, a stench that will not go away." For him it never did.

We watched them walk on, their eyes barely shifting from their fixed forward gaze as they passed two young people sitting on the ground. A man was comforting a woman who was sobbing quietly.

Aloma said to me, "I know that I would never have survived."

And I thought that Roman also knew this, and this was why it was hard for him to be with her here but I did not want to say this. And perhaps it was why he did not want to make the journey with my mother and both my sisters.

A year later in Auschwitz, with Fergal Keane, my father addressed a group of German school children. He told them he did not hold them to blame. They were, he said, building a new and better world. Father George, one of their teachers, said that he feels guilty.

"But why?" asked Fergal Keane. "You are not to blame. It had nothing to do with you."

"So it is. So it is," responded Father George. "Our German generation were guilty. It's a shadow, a shadow that will never leave us." The sins of the fathers will be visited on the children to the third and fourth generations. Or more. The author of Leviticus was not writing about guilt on this scale.

The watch towers and the barbed wire, the inmates' huts, the blown-apart gas chambers and their vacant desolation, all conjured images in my mind from elsewhere, not of the suffering that went on there. I found myself thinking of Georges Rouault's *Miserere* and of my father's paintings of his experiences. Yet it seemed inappropriate to be walking through Birkenau with my mind on paintings rather than the place itself.

And I was made conscious of how art is both an escape from thoughts of suffering and, at the same time, can serve as a focus for those thoughts. This is what icons do. Also because, as T.S.Eliot wrote, we "cannot bear very much reality". One latches onto an image – painting or photograph. It may help one stay at a point of reference. Yet, of course, both photographs and paintings constantly shift, change in our minds unless they, too, degenerate into symbols.

Krakow, clothes shop

59

STREET SCENE

We were in Krakow the evening after we visited Auschwitz. The weather was fair. The square and main streets were full of locals and tourists out in the cool, clear evening heading to the cafés and bars in the centre. Swifts arced overhead. We were walking along the shops on our way back from the centre to the hotel, having skirted close to the foot of the Castle. We must have appeared like tourists unwinding at the end of a day. We were hungry and the film crew were resting. Roman was carrying a walking stick because his knees were hurting and he was sunk in thoughts. He was angry.

Some young people, two men and a woman, possibly students, in high spirits but not drunk or dangerous, were walking towards us and skirted quite close to him. He swung out at them twice with his walking stick. Fortunately, he missed. It was as shocking as it was unexpected.

The students were so wrapped in their conversation that they barely seemed to notice. A woman on the opposite side of the road with a pale blue scarf and a bulging shopping bag turned to watch what she had seen in the reflection of a shop window. The busy, pleasant thoroughfare, the clear evening with the swifts circling high overhead against a sky of transparent cerulean blue tinged with the faintest yellow light, was this now for him an extension of Auschwitz?

Where was my father in his mind? His gesture of rage endorsed the impression that for him the present would always be overshadowed by the past. Half a century or a moment, they are thin as each other in the ever-rolling present.

I recalled him telling me once how in the soup queues in the ghetto the way to keep others away was a sharp punch to the jaw or rib. Sensing he wanted to be alone, I walked ahead of him. Turning, a little distance on, I saw the street reflected in the windows and Roman's figure in the glass of a shop selling garish women's clothes with mannequins in strong primary colours and others with broad black and white stripes. The violence of his outburst seemed to surround him, yet as I edged away to give him space I also felt ashamed of myself for moving from him. Ashamed and ashamed of him for his blind, irrational action.

60

CARRYING ON

Aloma was wondering if there was a point to our being here if Roman would not share his experiences with us. "Do you think it might have been different without Mark and June?"

I said that Roman was showing us what he could, and perhaps this was the only way he could communicate.

"Yes, I am not sure it would have been different without them here." Aloma added, despondently. "I hoped he would be able to include us. I thought we might be some consolation to him. That we could be with him and he with us. But he cannot."

"Could have doesn't help us. We've seen most of the places he went."[1] "And we can see the depth of his pain. Perhaps with a different film team it might have... Perhaps doesn't help either."

"I know, but he makes me feel that I am an intruder. How can I edit his book if he doesn't allow me to ask him questions? How can I know what is an error and what is an inconsistency if he will not answer? In his escape women were a burden, an encumbrance. On this journey I am also a problem for him, like those women, weaker, more vulnerable. He resents my questions. He resents my being here."

"I don't think he resents your being here," I replied, though wondering if perhaps he did, or if resent was the right word.

"He was alone from 1942 till the end of the war. He lived and survived alone. Coming back to this he is alone in his mind. That is how he faced it then and how he sees it now. I think he has no energy to relate what he feels other than in the way he does for the camera, in a public way – that is his private voice too."

"Yes, but we are being distanced by him. At least, I mean, from his experience. Aren't we?"

We could only be distanced. Would the absence of cameras really have made a difference? The gap between what he said and what he saw, between lens and whatever it was they were filming, those gaps dispel any illusory certainty that what is seen is what can be known.

61

DRESDEN

From Krakow we drove west into Germany to Dresden where Roman worked as a slave labourer making bullet cartridges in the basement of a cigarette factory on 68 Schandauer Strasse. The place is still a cigarette factory. But the management would not let us in to see the basement – there were consultations while we waited and then our request was politely but firmly declined. It was in that basement that Roman and the other slave labourers had heard and seen the Allied bombings through the small windows up to the ground level, and rejoiced as they saw the SS guards cowering in fear. He and the other slave-labourers learned the difference between the sounds of high explosive bombs and the incendiary bombs that caused the firestorms.

We waited for what seemed a long time on the street in the sunshine while continuity footage was filmed. The churches one could see, those remaining from prewar times sixty-five years earlier, had scorched steeples blackened to the very spires. It was hard to imagine flames licking so high during the firestorms or visualize the slave-labourers making their way down to the River Elbe, led by Chimowicz. On his advice they cloaked themselves with blankets soaked in chilled water before they left the factory. In this way the Jewish slave-labourers survived the smoke and flames. I tried to imagine them lying flat on the road surface, covered by their blankets, as fireballs cartwheeled over them, or as they walked on down to the Elbe seeing the civilians of Dresden jumping from upper floors of burning apartments – but just as I am writing these words and know that they do not convey the blazing horror, so too they could not really permeate my mind in Dresden on a warm May morning.

The spires were the colour of trees in a Max Ernst painting, burnt red-black against a pale cerulean sky with surreal wispy white clouds.

We drove to the leafy village of Oberpoyritz, some fifteen minutes' drive out of Dresden, looking for the home of Mrs Herta Fuchs. It was there in her garden shed that my father had stayed for three or four weeks after his escape from a death march from Dresden, following the Allied bombings there on 13th and 14th of February 1945. Roman had visited her here late in her life. They were photographed together and those photos had appeared in a UK national newspaper Sunday colour-supplement under the title *The Kindness of Strangers*. He had helped her financially and applied to Yad Vashem to name her as one of The Righteous Gentiles, those honoured by the State of Israel for risking their lives to help Jewish men, women and children during the *Shoah*. The article described how she had given refuge to him and two others who escaped the death march, for which eventually her husband paid with his life. There is a plaque in her name in the Avenue of the Righteous Gentiles at Yad Vashem. She was too old to attend the ceremony to mark the occasion, but one was organised in Germany in her honour.

Roman led us to a charming cottage separated from an open field by a lane, a ditch and a cherry tree. Sweet peas climbed the walls and there were raised small rectangular vegetable beds. For her last twenty years she had worked as a washerwoman, using one of its few small outhouses with washing vats. Just as I was trying to imagine my father in this lovely environment, he told us that this was not the place where he was given shelter after his escape from the death march.

Now Roman directed us to Mrs Fuchs's original home a couple of minutes' drive away. We parked the cars at the end of a narrow, asphalted lane, signposted neatly, with lawns and flowerbeds and not a blade or blossom out of place. Roman looked for the garden shed where he had slept and lived during the weeks he worked for Herr and Frau Fuchs, where his duties involved tending their vegetable patch. The owner of the home emerged. She wanted no filming and us gone. Mark and June hung about a little down the lane, cameras and boom at the ready. We saw a shed that Roman did not think was *that* shed. It was about the right size, he said. Just a garden shed: two by one-and-a-half metres with a pitched roof. A shed.

With those proportions firmly in my mind, we drove a few minutes to Pillnitz Schloss, the elegant summer residence of Frederick Augustus I of Saxony. His *Wasserpalais* on the Elbe, designed and decorated throughout in the baroque Chinoiserie fashion of the early 18th century. It was the work of Matthäus Daniel Pöppelmann and Zacharias Longuelune, a delicately proportioned fusion of the Baroque palatial style and Meissen porcelain Chinoiserie.

How easily the mind accepts such transitions. The elegant formal gardens in the English style (pre-Lancelot "Capability" Brown), the orangery, stately spreading plane trees, all these had already been beautifully restored following the massive floods of 2002. It was a good place to sit and talk, but we did not talk. Instead, we wandered about like five threads occasionally interweaving, saying a few words, parting, heading to the terraces overlooking the Elbe, meandering in tighter curves than the river beyond the Schloss, wandering in the sunshine, between the other tourists and then back to the shade of the plane trees.

From a bench, I gazed at the delicate modelled foliage and figures on the columns, capitals and cornices. The work was so fine it could have been painted by porcelain experts. It was detailed with the sort of vitality characterizing the work of those celebrating the discovery of a style, unlike for instance the later institutionalised patterns that churn style into the dull industry marking Wedgewood's work three decades later.

I found myself trying to recall a piece of prose. It was by Geoffrey Hill. I remembered the passage in question as relating to the gap in time between an event and its recollection – the spreading space between what has happened and how it is seen. I wished that I had it with me. It seemed important to have it then. I thought it related directly to something I was trying to understand but could not express.

On returning home I dug it out. It is the final paragraph from the end of Geoffrey Hill's early volume of poems *King Log* (André Deutsch, London, 1968) from the two-page essay *Funeral Music* in the section subtitled *King Stork*.

> There is a distant fury of battle. Without attempting factual detail, I had in mind the Battle of Towton, fought on Palm Sunday, 1461. It is now customary to play down the violence of the Wars of the Roses and to present them as dynastic skirmishes fatal, perhaps, to the old aristocracy but generally of small concern to the common people and without much effect on the economic routines of the kingdom. Statistically, this may be arguable; imaginatively, the Battle of Towton itself commands one's belated witness. In the accounts of the contemporary chroniclers it was a holocaust. Some scholars have suggested that the claims were exaggerated, although the military, Colonel A. H. Burne, argues convincingly for the reasonableness of the early estimates. He reckons that over 26,000 men died at Towton and remarks that "the scene must have beggared description and its very horror probably deterred the survivors from passing on stories of the fight". Even so, one finds the chronicler of Croyland Abbey writing that the blood of the slain lay caked with the snow which covered the ground and that, when the snow melted, the blood flowed along the furrows and ditches for a distance of two or three miles.

The passage's particular charge owes much to the writer's consciousness of distance and delay, the delayed release of the blood as it melted well after the time of battle and its subsequent spread miles beyond the battle-ground. "There is a distant fury of battle." There are, in fact, two senses to "distant" here: the distance covered by the blood and the distance in time as the writer contemplates these events.

What was I really thinking then in Pillnitz Schloss, looking at the pastel Chinoiserie tracery? Was it anything more than a general sense of dislocation? The ashes from the alternating centrifugal, centripetal firestorms in Dresden a few kilometres away across the Elbe must have powdered this Baroque residence like surreal off-coloured icing sugar on a fine confection.

Pillnitz Schloss

62

THE ESCAPE FROM THE FOREST – VERSION 1

Back to Pillnitz, wandering around in the surreal calm of the Baroque *schloss* and gardens, separately, each with his or her own thoughts.

Then our paths crossed and Aloma and I sat down on a bench. I cannot recall our conversation exactly and wish I had recorded it but the gist of it was that things did not add up. They did not make sense. Throughout the trip Roman's memory had been very precise, sequential, sharp. And here, in Oberpoyritz, it was different. The sequence of his account was jumbled. He was staccato in his responses, he was boiling inside. We could not understand quite what had happened. Points did not tally. Why?

It took time for me to discover the answer. On that journey we did not find out, not everything. Now I think I know as much as I am likely to. It is 2014, nine years later. To understand why there were several versions of his escape from the Death March, and of his time with Frau Herta Fuchs, it is necessary to go back and compare the accounts. In so doing I came to understand Roman better and only truly did so after he was no longer alive. My father died in 2012.

In that first version, written before our 2005 trip to Poland and

Dresden, the slave-labourer metal workers have all been led out of the blazing city of Dresden on a Death March. At an overnight encampment my father overhears some of the toughest older men – men in their late twenties and early thirties – talking of an escape. They are afraid that they may all soon be shot in some ditch. They have witnessed stragglers, the sick, the older members of their group shot, and they have seen the particular viciousness of one female SS guard, Gul, who shot one of the more compassionate German managers who wanted to keep the metal workers in the factory in Dresden in defiance of received orders. Gul shot him point blank in the factory toilet.

Desperate to join the escape group Roman promised Moniek, the leader, that he could get them civilian clothes in the factory back in Dresden. Since they were all marked as Jewish prisoners with a broad white stripe painted down their backs and a "louse alley", a line shaved down the middle of their heads, civilian clothes and a haircut would be key to survival after any escape. Dressed as they were and looking as they did, they could go nowhere without being captured and killed. Roman's promise is desperate. It is a lie. But it is plausible since Roman's job at the munitions factory in the basement in Dresden was as a *Läufer*, a runner, between the various departments. He would have known everyone and where everything was. So, after deliberating, they agreed to take him.

That evening he is the last to escape from the open compound with relatively few guards and, following the instructions of the leader of the escapees, he carries his clogs and runs zig-zag to the forest nearby across a road.

Up to this point the first and second versions match. The narrative is vivid in its detail. Given the clarity of my father's recall, there is no reason why his memory would stall and detail fade at this crucial moment when he meets up with the others in the forest. Roman runs into the forest, bewildered, on his own. For the first time in five years, he is free, but still in danger of his life.

But from this point onwards, in the forest, the versions differ significantly. Version one before our trip to Poland, version two, that appeared in his book *Roman's Journey*. Now what happens in version one?

After what seems a long wait in the forest, Roman meets up with two of the other escapees, Avraham Sztajer and Adam Szwajcer. In the account there is no further mention of all the others who have escaped: Moniek the Boxer, Moniek the Testicle, Franz or the three women who all featured up to this point. They simply drop out of the story. In this first version Avraham Sztajer and Adam Szwajcer tell Roman to go down to into Oberpoyritz, a village they see beyond the forest. He does this. He knocks on a door and asks if the people will take both him and Avraham and Adam in. In this account Avraham Sztajer and Adam Szwajcer watch and wait from the safety of the trees as my father meets Mrs Herta Fuchs and finds them all shelter.

Of course, this first version is entirely implausible – they did not know who lived there and the Germans in that neat little village answering my father's knock on the door in the middle of the night would have called the home guard or the SS and then, in all likelihood, he and the others would have been shot. In this version the other escapees disappear from the account. What happened to them? How did Avraham Sztajer and Adam Szwajcer escape? What was the connection that brought them to Mr and Mrs Fuchs in Oberpoyritz? None of this was clear in the first version. Dozens of details fail to add up.

After much questioning by Aloma, Roman sat down in London after our journey and wrote the second version. The point at which the two versions converge and tally is after my father had stayed with Frau and Herr Fuchs, living in their garden shed for three or four weeks, working for them. Sztajer and Szwajcer stay with them and work for a farmer nearby, Roman returns to his home town in Poland by bicycle and seven weeks later returns to Dresden bearing gifts for the Fuchses – soap, coffee, sugar and smoked meat, profits from black-market transactions he had made. Herta Fuchs is dressed in black, her husband and Swajcer have been shot by Russians loyal to

Vlasov a Russian pro-fascist general, spurred by local Germans from Oberpoyritz. Sztajer has escaped.

In 1989 Mrs Fuchs was living in miserable poverty. Her home had been confiscated and given to a Stasi member. She was eking out a very basic existence, bringing in water from an outside tap, suffering from the cold in winter. A local teacher, Elke Preusser, wrote to Yad VaShem on her behalf and traced my father. She wrote to him on Herta Fuchs's behalf. Then Roman flew to meet her. He wrote about the encounter and that piece was the basis for the long article that appeared in one of the British Sunday supplements entitled *The Kindness of Strangers*. And it is what my father sent to Yad VaShem where a plaque in the Avenue of the Righteous marks her name. In the article my father wrote:

> I was delighted to have found her. I remembered my time of March and April 1945 with feelings of deep gratitude when I was with her and her husband. It was understood then by every German that hiding a Jew was punishable by death. Mr and Mrs Fuchs not only sheltered me but also Sztajer and Szwajcer.
>
> They had nothing whatsoever to gain from it; we had nothing to give them but gratitude. Why had they sheltered us? Would I have the courage, the strength of humanity to save another being? Would I stake my life for someone? For a stranger?... I should now like to believe that I would. Perhaps after their example, the way they saved me, I too might act courageously. I also know that it is so much easier to say what one would do but quite another matter to actually do it. They paid for the great, humane and brave act with Mr Fuch's life.

Donations to Mrs Fuchs streamed in to the newspaper from around Britain, including an alpaca coat from one particularly generous reader.

Our questions concerning the first version were unavoidable yet they were met with coolness or a look that said: "Why are you causing me pain?"

63

A MEETING WITH AVRAHAM SZTAJER

In 2002 my father was interviewed by Dr Michal Unger who was researching for a book she was writing on the Lodz ghetto. Roman asked her about Avraham Sztajer and she told him that Sztajer was living in Tel Aviv and gave him his phone number. A meeting was arranged at a sparsely furnished apartment he or his daughter Hava Shnitzki owned north of Netanya overlooking the sea. Driving there I asked my father what he hoped to find out from Avraham Sztajer.

How he escaped. How he managed to get away when Mr Fuchs and Adam Szwajcer were shot. What did Sztajer tell the Russian soldiers. Why did they not shoot him? Then he was silent, deep in thought.

From this I inferred that my father knew that Avraham Sztajer had been there when Fuchs and Szwajcer were shot and not *somewhere else at the time*, as my father wrote in the first version. Apparently, Roman simply wrote those words to bridge the account, a sort of imaginative connecting-piece in the text. At this point in time, two years before we visited Poland, I did not have reason to doubt the first version and accepted inconsistencies or lacunae as his way of telling his story. But it set me thinking.

It was a bright day. Sunlight streamed into the apartment from the balcony on the fifth or sixth floor overlooking the smooth Mediterranean with even smoother darker currents streaking the surface.

Sztajer and Roman shook hands. Sztajer was a solid, strongly built man in his eighties, very slightly stooped but with a firm handshake and a keen glance that assessed a person's worth and whether to waste time on them. He was interested but not cordial. He owned property in Netanya and Tel Aviv. Sztajer and my father scoured each other to find in the man before them the face they remembered from back in Oberpoyritz.

Sztajer's expression was cool and, it seemed to me, even slightly contemptuous. Why the disdain? Despite this, Sztajer had agreed to the meeting, so clearly his curiosity had been aroused. What did he want to find out at this meeting? The way they met – it didn't have the feel of a reunion. To my disappointment he and my father chose to speak to each other in Polish which neither Sztajer's daughter nor I spoke. It was clear from his body language that Sztajer felt no debt of gratitude. He owed my father nothing. Nor was he going to explain or reveal anything.

This was not a man who would have relied on a relatively inexperienced youngster knocking on the door of an unknown German house in a village he had never visited, looking to find refuge for himself and two others hiding in the forest. He would not have entrusted his fate to my father. The version my father had written did not square with this man. Even thought they spoke in Polish, ignoring us, after a few minutes, Avraham Sztajer asked us to leave them to talk on their own. His daughter and I sat on white plastic chairs on the balcony overlooking the sea. We sat in silence. I should have asked her what version she knew of the escape, if her father ever spoken about this or if he had ever mentioned my father. But I did not.

After five minutes I saw Sztajer rise to his feet. The meeting was over. There were no words to suggest there would be a further meeting. Their handshake was more cursory than on arrival.

Driving back, my father was pensive.

"Did Sztajer tell you what you hoped to find out?" I asked as we cornered the cliff at Zukei Yam.

He shook his head.

64

THE SAME EYES

Weighing, commenting on or even comparing the versions my father wrote concerning his escape I cannot help feeling guilty in some measure, because to analyse or criticise implies, in some measure, to judge. I have no right to judge my father for how he acted during the Shoah. It is not possible to know how you or I would have behaved under those circumstances unless we were *there*. At least I do not know. Yet since he asked me, and then Aloma, to read and edit all his drafts, and out of love and support we did so, I cannot help recognise the major differences between the versions and, by implication, what this tells me about my father.

The Second Version and other things that surfaced at the end of his life and after his death helped me understand him better. One of them was the discovery of three half-siblings, roughly my own age, about whose existence I had previously known nothing. I discovered this a year before the end of his life, while I was visiting London for a week, my father suggested that I meet a couple, husband and wife he had met at a swimming pool "with whom I might have a lot in common." So I went there unprepared and within a few minutes, I saw in her face, eyes like my father's and Aloma's. "It is what you are thinking..." she said. I am not sure how long I sat there in silence. My mind swam. Here I was in my fifties, meeting a sister I never knew existed – and the experience was for both of us completely surreal and, at the same time, it also felt quite natural, as unremarkable as two people sitting, drinking tea or coffee out of mugs at a round wooden table and then going for a walk. This was not a film with music, with climactic moments, no confession, no preparation, trail of clues, not the steady build-up of plot, just two strangers meeting in middle age, one to discover a half-brother, the other a half-sister.

We met in her home near Hampstead Heath, a warm, creative generous house with many stairs, armchairs, and books, books everywhere. Then we went for a walk, up towards Kenwood and as I looked east towards the ponds and banked trees up to Highgate and the spire of St Michael's I thought how strange it was that my own half-sister now lived just two miles from where I had grown up and how we had possibly passed each other in the street, or here on Hampstead Heath, stood behind each other in a shop, each in his and her own world, knowing nothing about the other.

She chose to have next to no contact with my father, her genetic father and her sister and brother even less. After his death I found five of six postcards and short letters from her to him.

Our conversation was easy-going. But deep down the waters were churning, more within her, I sensed, than in me. This knowledge and status was probably harder for her than me, I thought. I had grown up with my biological father, she had not. There was much we had in common but the gulf in time was unbridgeable. You cannot construct a common past that has not existed. We agreed to meet from time to time. A year later, I sent her an email to invite her to my father – to our father's funeral. I invited her and through her, her sister and brother to the memorial service a year later. I did not see her and her sister arrive. They came late, sat at the back and left early. Their brother, my half-brother, the half-brother I have never met, did not come.

Do I resemble him, I wondered? On so many occasions people had said to me that they had thought that they had seen me a few days, weeks or a month back in London – at a time when I had not been in London. Could this have been my half-brother, who lived in a different town in the south of England but who possibly visited his own sisters from time to time, or came to London for work? Or might it be yet another brother who neither he nor I were aware of? The discovery made me wonder if there was not an entire secret world in the present. Had it been there to see all along?

Another discovery was the strange and hurtful revelation that my father had taken credit for major stained-glass projects I had designed and made – in Rwanda and St Johns Wood Synagogue. These were projects in which he had not been involved.

And the third discovery was the second version of his escape.

65

THE ESCAPE – THE SECOND VERSION

Now, when I look again at that second published version in *Roman's Journey*, the version RH wrote after our journey to Poland in 2004, my questions and comments are inserted not with a view to judging my late father (how much harsher this seems now that he is no longer alive to answer, rebuke or rage) but in order better to understand the complexity of the burden he carried in his mind all those years. He must have felt intense guilt for the deaths of those who escaped with him. Though many survivors experienced guilt simply *for having survived* when so many of their families and friends did not, for my father that sense was compounded by what happened during the escape he was allowed to join.

Roman enters the forest and immediately Moniek the Boxer, the leader of the escape group, catches hold of him. They are nine people in all, including three women, partners of three of the men. They cover half the distance back to Dresden on foot, walking along the main road, since had they been found in the forest they would have been shot without question. They are stopped by home guards manning anti-tank guns. One of their group is a former pilot, Franz, one of whose grandparents was discovered to be Jewish. He chats to the guards in perfect German and they continue on their way.

Explaining that he has to shift the group of prisoners Franz somehow gets them onto the first tram to Dresden. They reach the cigarette factory – the munitions workshops had been in the basement – and climb up to the second floor and then lower themselves by rope on to the top of two of the huge tobacco vats to hide, the pungent smell of tobacco protecting them from the search dogs should the SS come to look for them. One of the women is too ill to be taken up onto the roof and is left in one of the abandoned cars outside.

My father writes that later in the day they hear the SS next door and the woman's screams. They all stay atop the tobacco vats, not descending from them even to urinate. Next day the SS return with dogs. The odour of tobacco prevents the dogs from sniffing them. A day later the SS return once more and search the metal factory in the basement, where they had worked as slave-labourers. Then the boxer allows them down for the first time to defecate and drink. On the morning of the third day my father writes that the group leader Moniek helps him to descend to the factory side to get them all clothes, as he had promised.

He meets a person, not hitherto mentioned in the narrative, called "the Dutchman" who goes to get Herr Braun, the factory manager. Then Braun fits my father with a pair of galoshes, socks, a Tyrolean jacket and trousers. His hair is cut short. He is given some food and a typed note and an address in Oberpoyritz a village outside Dresden where he is told he will be able to stay with Herr and Frau Fuchs.

On two occasions my father mentioned to me that Herta Fuchs had been the mistress of Czarnula whose seniority led my father to believe that he was an SS officer although in the book his precise office and rank are not detailed. Czarnula first appears in *Roman's Journey* on page 157 "in Stutthof... wearing a long black leather coat... together with army men and a few SS." According to my father – and again this is not recorded in the book – Czarnula had several mistresses around Dresden. He is seen to appear at the Fuchs home twice (p. 192 of *Roman's Journey*) which would seem to confirm the possibility that Mrs Fuchs was his mistress. If this were the case, then the order to send Roman to work for Herta Fuchs would have come not from Braun but from Czarnula, for two reasons. First, as a favour, a gift to his mistress of an unpaid domestic worker. And secondly, since the war was faring disastrously for the Germans with the Soviets rapidly advancing across Poland and into Germany, saving the lives of a few Jews might prove a useful card to protect him in future. And this too might explain how Sztajer and Szwajcer also managed to find refuge with the Fuchses.

In my father's compelling and flowing narrative there are a number of conundrums. It is not clear how Mr Braun, the German civilian manager of the metal factory, would have known about the Fuchses, simple folk, villagers living across the Elbe, a few miles outside of Dresden. There is no mention anywhere of a family or childhood connection between Czarnula or Herr Braun and Mr or Mrs Fuchs.

In my father's book, the conversation between him and Mr Braun and the Dutchman forms a continuity passage, but logically it does not add up.

"I was given the address of Mr and Mrs Fuchs and then told to memorize and destroy it.... If anyone stopped me on the road, I should show [...] the paper the Dutchman was typing and explain that [...] I was now going to work for a farmer in Oberpoyritz.

'When they question you, say you don't understand and keep repeating the same story over and over again. Don't tell them anything about the factory or any of us.'

'Will you help my friends?' I asked anxiously. 'They also need clothes and food, and help to escape...'

'Yes, yes, don't worry about that...'

'They're on the roof,' I said.

All seemed to be going well, though I didn't have a chance to say goodbye to the others. In fact I was really terrified of Moniek the Testicle, so I was glad not to have to face him just yet."

Up to that point he has not spoken to Mr Braun or to the Dutchman about his fellow escapees. He did not mention them once to the factory director or to the clerk. Yet now in what Roman presents as a caring comment, just as he was about to leave, he sought help for them and, at the same time revealed their location, hidden on the roof. He failed to obtain clothes for his fellow escapees and now he has revealed their hiding place. So it is down to Braun to help the other escapees. Or perhaps it is not just Braun in the picture, but also Czarnula, directing my father to Herta Fuchs. In which case my father has told not just Braun but also Czarnula about the other escapees hidden on the tobacco vats. And if my father thought Czarnula was in the SS (and Czarnula was not, as I discovered later from Chanan Werbejczyk) then the revelation is all the more serious and will condemn those men to death.

The conversation in my father's narrative is pacifying, smoothing in its simplicity. This is one of the most painful moments in the book. He is about to step free (though still facing potential dangers), he has an alias and a formal typed document to support his new name, his hair has been cut, he is dressed now in good Austro-German clothing. He has a food parcel and is off to an address that should provide him with refuge. Yet the others are there, hiding on the tobacco vats.

"'Will you help my friends?' I asked anxiously. 'They also need clothes and food, and help to escape.'

'Yes, yes, don't worry about that...'"

Mollifying, helping to gloss over this crux in his life and in the story. "Don't worry." Then or in the future. "Don't worry." You did what you could. There is nothing more to do about it. *Don't worry*. Enabling him to tell part of what happened, as much as he could face, enough to carry the narrative, a narrative that on a certain level of his being he could live with. This is balanced by confessional openness, disarming candour at key moments in the account of the escape. This may be a case where if my father admits to one thing, he thereby wins understanding and sympathy. And in the process another is overlooked:

"I told a lie. I said that Mr Braun and the others at the Dresden office had promised me that if I escaped with them the office people would help us find civilian clothes." [p.175]; "Will you help my friends…. They also need clothes and food, and help to escape."

But of the seven, so far as my father was aware, only two others escaped from Dresden: Sztajer and Szwajcer. The rest, he had to assume, were killed. Was the price of my father's escape the death of the others? He was offered freedom but was unable to help the others. Were the words "Will you help my friends?" caring, or were they the death-ticket for those others? Where was Czarnula during that conversation? How did Sztajer and Szwajcer escape? Were they part of the nine men and women who escaped into the forest? This was not clear from the second version. At that meeting in Netanya in 2002 there were three questions my father had ready for Sztajer. First, he wanted (and perhaps dreaded) to learn from a first-hand source what had happened to the others waiting on the tobacco vats for the civilian clothes he had promised them. Secondly, he was keen to know how it was that Sztajer and Szwjacer came to be sent to the Fuchses' house a week or so after he had arrived there. The third question was how Sztajer had managed to evade death again at Oberpoyritz, later, when both Mr Fuchs and Szwaycer were shot.

Yet Avraham Sztajer did not provide my father with any of those answers. I think that there in that room, lit by the pool of western light from the sea, they were back in Oberpoyritz as though it was 57 years earlier and Sztajer and my father each kept key details from the other. Did he accuse my father of failing to provide the escapees with civilian clothes? Was that spoken about at all? Or was Sztajer never part of that escape. Was he somewhere else at the time? Did my father not speak to Sztajer about this because all those years he bore within him feelings of guilt for the death of the others? Did he and Szwajcer manage to stay in Dresden when the others were marched away? Was his story quite different?

66

THE PROMISE

My father made a promise he could not keep in order to live. Survival was an hour-by-hour business, day by day. When he promised those civilian clothes, he did so in order to survive imminent death. On the Death March he could have been killed at any moment – by rife-shot in some gulley or pit, just as the sick and the stragglers on the forced-march column had been summarily shot along the way. A bullet to the back of the head. It was this that they all feared at that moment. He saw the group planning the escape as his only chance. He would have promised anything to be included. What was hard for my father to face was the consequence of that lie. The promise he made came good only for him – until, that is, he saw Szwajcer and Sztajer. If they indeed had been part of the escape to the forest, then their presence in Oberpoyritz made his failure to act less terrible. It *had* been possible for the others to escape too. It must have been. But Sztajer was a living reminder of his failure to make good on his promise.

    The second narrative makes better sense but it still does not add up. If, as he told me, Herta Fuchs was one of Czarnula's mistresses, then why does this not enter into the written text? The answer is complex and central to my father's attitude to life after the war, and to his own extended persona, which is to say the person he grew to be through his words and conduct. I tracked the list of all names of SS officers on the internet. There was not a single mention of Erich Czarnula. He was not in the SS but a powerful civilian, working under orders from Hans Biebow, the Nazi administrative head of the Lodz Ghetto, a former coffee dealer from Bremen who had the ear of Gauleiter Arthur Greiser.

By not associating Herta Fuchs as Czarnula's mistress, Roman makes her and Mr Fuchs appear altruistic. Their actions are not presented as the consequence of compulsion, the sort of gift that could not be refused, a favour, wanted or unwanted, but the *kindness of strangers*. Herr and Frau Fuchs housed three Jewish men at considerable risk to their own lives. But what if they had no option? What if they were compelled to accept the "favour" of a senior official who sent Roman to them and then the other two, Sztajer and Szwajcer, in order to notch up a creditable act to help Czarnula save his own skin when the Russians or Americans came? Roman was in two minds as to whether to describe Czarnula as an SS man or as a sort of Oskar Schindler figure, caring for the *Metalabteilung* workers, protecting them and saving lives.

So long as the Reich stood and so long as Czarnula wielded authority then the Fuchses were under his protection. When the Reich fell, they would be in danger either way, potentially under threat from ex-Nazis for acting altruistically and sheltering Jews; or after the war they would be in danger having previously enjoyed special privileges thanks to Mrs Fuchs's connection to Czarnula.

Of the meeting with Sztajer and Szwajcer my father writes:

"They seemed pleasantly amused to see me. They seemed relaxed and spoke quite freely. They were working for another farmer who lived nearby, but they said that they came to the Fuchses each night (but I think that they must have slept on the farm where they worked.) [...] They told me that Mr Braun had also written them a letter of recommendation with the address of the farm. They had been told I was at the Fuchses.

I asked Sztajer and Szwajcer what had happened to the others in the factory with whom I escaped, Moniek the Boxer, for example. Adam Szwajcer said that Czarnula told them – at this point Sztajer interrupted him and said: 'Oh, you'll meet up with them in Heaven.'"

My father believed that the escapees had all died because he had failed to keep his promise. The last sentence: "Adam Szwajcer said that Czarnula told them – at this point Sztajer interrupted him and said, "Oh, you'll meet up with them in Heaven.""

This brutal line "Oh, you'll meet up with them in Heaven" in effect closes the door on further possible information concerning the fate of the others in the factory. By the time my father wrote the above version, Avraham Sztajer was dead too. He died in 2003. And we do not know whether they were part of the escape or not, or how Czarnula told them... or what he told them. The line elides the full story, either because my father did not know it or because he did not want to elaborate.

To me those words in the published version do not ring true. Yet they are consonant with my father's need to be generous, to himself, to humanity and to others for the rest of his life. He was one of the most generous people I have known. He gave away many of his paintings. He gave people his time and refused to accept payment for most of the commemorative projects in which he was involved. This munificence caused many to think him wealthy.

67

THE KINDNESS OF STRANGERS

Thereafter, whenever he spoke or wrote of her, to my father Herta Fuchs had acted purely altruistically. This story, this picture gathered permanence. He knew (but never said) that she had been trapped in impossible circumstances. He elected to empathize with her. She had sheltered three Jews and was widowed either because of this or because neighbours, jealous of the *proteczja* she had enjoyed through Czarnula, had informed on her to the Russians.

To my father it mattered not why Herta Fuchs had suffered but that she *had* suffered. She had helped him and he chose to put the kindest interpretation on that help. So it became a selfless act. And when he met her he saw a broken old woman in severely reduced circumstances. Here was someone he could help. The manner in which he lionized her cause, wrote to the newspapers, contacted Yad VaShem to inscribe her as a *Righteous Among The Nations* showed him at his most gracious and generous. And to some degree, his forgiveness and understanding empowered him. He bypassed some details of the original story. Now he was the survivor and she the altruistic person who had helped him survive. Meeting in the 1990s, communicating person to person recorded and repeated in news articles and on film until this version superseded the grey tones of what had happened, giving it the noblest complexion. In an English

Christian way it helped him too. His generosity gave his disturbed conscience a measure of calm, or for want of a better word, of absolution. One marvelled at his lack of rancour and his kindness. He melded his past and his present into a persona heroically refined and exemplary in its humanism.

The manner of his narrative was embraced by the British society he had adopted and which, he gratefully acknowledged, had adopted him. The narrative he told in the many radio, television and news interviews, the persona he projected was of one who has suffered, who despite all he experienced celebrates life, shares his experiences without hatred or any desire for vengeance.

68

MOVING ASHES

Twenty years ago I designed the Shoah memorial at Kibbutz Maagan Michael in Israel, commemorating the members of the kibbutz whose families had been murdered during the Shoah. There were surprisingly many names to include, until one realises that several cases involve almost entire families. It is a simple memorial: six massive square stones piled in a column, each stone rotated 45 degrees, so that the corners project. Kibbutz members place flowers directly on the stone or in small vases on those corners. Some leave memorial pebbles. Each stone has two rough-hewn sides and two smooth-faced sides on which the names are chiselled. The column is surrounded on all four sides by a solid stone seat, facing in to it and recessed from it by about three metres. Groups can gather within the contained space, descending to it through steps in the centre of one of the four sides.

At the foot of the memorial is a bronze plaque, cast by my father. It serves as the lid to an urn made by Asnat, my wife. It simply states in Hebrew that the urn contains ashes of victims from the concentration camps. What is ash but transposed carbon? That is the power of Primo Levi's story from *The Periodic Table* in which the atom of carbon becomes, eventually, the writer's own final full-stop.

Yet the physical presence of those ashes, once one has read the lid of the urn, compels a transposition of thought. What am I saying? Just that once you have read it, you become aware that a group of 17-year olds have cared to carry those ashes, the jumbled human remains gathered from the site of an extermination camp. Those ashes, properly speaking, prevent the memorial from being a cenotaph. The memorial is not hollow and not empty. That the carbon there in the urn was, were once people just like themselves.

69

HOW MUCH IS TOO MUCH?

The phrase "it does not bear thinking about" informs of the human instinct for both self-deception and self-preservation.

During our journey, increasingly I found myself asking: How much should a person know? Does knowledge of this subject cauterize as much as it sensitizes? How much detail should go into the telling?

Stephen and James Smith, who created Beit Shalom, the first Holocaust memorial museum in Nottingham, as well as the National Genocide Memorial Centre in Rwanda, contend that the more a person knows and the more people there are who learn about genocide, the greater is the chance of preventing it in the future. Education can set people on a different tangent, nudge them in such a way that later in life, when conditions and circumstances of killing may arise in the face of incitement, they will respond differently. The Smith brothers believe the world is now too small for its deeds to go unheard.

In Rwanda, when I saw the stream of thousands of visitors in Kigali to the memorial centre, not only victims but the families of the perpetrators, I came to share the Smith brothers' belief that knowledge can help to steer us against neutrality or indifference to the plight of others. I want to hope that knowledge can steer people away from their worst instincts, making them conscious of intolerance, of prejudice, of recognizing the plight of strangers in our midst.

I asked my father: "How much information do you think it appropriate to impart when talking to another person or to an audience on this subject? Should there be a degree of self-censorship?"

My father's head tilted slightly and his brows lifted inquiringly. "What exactly do you mean?"

I could only clarify it by offering two examples for him to consider.

In the first example two young girls are brutally murdered. This is reported in the media; including police statements and eyewitness accounts, maps, diagrams of the crime scene and photos of the girls when they were alive. The story continues as the details emerge. We follow it for all the reasons we read news stories: curiosity, prurience, habit, the desire for information. Once our mental files are updated, we move on.

However, now that the information is clear, would you wish to find out more about the case if you could? If additional photos from the scene of the crime were available, would you seek them out or avoid them? Does every gram of evidence add to the total sum of knowledge? How much is enough information? "Enough", of course, is a fluid entity, differing from individual to individual, the epoch they live, and how close acceptable moeurs permit them to get to the gore. During the French revolution, for example, there was a point when the mass attendance at guillotine executions dwindled to an indifferent quorum. The spectacle had become repetitive, perhaps to the point of boredom.

Another example, this time not hypothetical: the genocide in Rwanda, a hundred frenzied days in 1994. Many, gathered into churches and schools, were killed by fire, grenade and machine-gun. In the main, however, the killing was piecemeal, in homes, banana plantations, fields, at crossroads. Most of the killers used machetes or clubs or sticks with nails driven into the end, primitive tools prepared in advance for use against one's neighbour, tools to hand, implements prepared or quickly knocked together for lethal purpose. How much more do you or I wish or need to know?

There is a piece of documentary film of a small crossroads somewhere in Rwanda, where Hutu *interahamwe* thugs club one person after another to death, then rest leaning on their clubs and sticks, panting, wiping their brows from time to time because killing is a tiring job.

The above scene was filmed, by chance, with a telephoto lens partially hidden from the killers' view by some trees at a distance of perhaps 200 metres from the scene of the killings. Almost unbelievably, this footage was continuously screened in 2004, and may still be for all I know, at Kigali airport departure lounge close by the duty-free shops selling Rwandan coffee and conical basketwork in the shape of rural huts. It is grainy footage. You need more than a moment to realise what you are seeing. The unfolding activity does not, at first, seem credible or possible.

Would it have helped us to comprehend more, better to understand the Rwandan genocide, if the camera lens would have had a stronger, crisper zoom? How close do we need to be? Again, one asks, how many details do we need to know? Do we need to see the gash made by the machete in the victim's skull?

So when I asked Roman, how much we need to know, I was really making two points. There was the thought that had stirred within me from the time of my visit to Rwanda in 2004 and then a year later in Poland; the consideration that excessively detailed knowledge of this subject could harm a person. There may be limits to what an individual should allow him or herself to know or to hear.

Secondly, I was really saying, overtly hinting, that I could hear no more. Macbeth's words: "I have supped full of horrors", are very hard to relay to a survivor when it is he who has seen them and you who have merely listened. There are limits to duty. This was the third point, one I found difficult to say to my father – limits to his duty to tell and ours to hear.

Now, with the intensity of the visit to Poland, I needed to be able to sit down to a meal, to travel, to be with my father without hearing more. There were times in the day when I needed to know that it would not be necessary to raise my inner defences. And now that he is dead, I miss him. He died in 2012. I miss his laughter, his capricious humour. I miss him in many ways and I hear his voice. But I do not miss hearing him speak of the Shoah.

70

BOOK WITHOUT SHELF

For my father the Shoah was his life's trauma.

If memory is like a library, then trauma is a book that cannot be properly bound and will never find a shelf. It is forever loose, unsettled, beating about the brain. It cannot rest. It is always present, forever troubling.

When a person experiences trauma, he or she is encouraged to speak to professionals, psychologists or counsellors to offload the burden of the heart. In my father's case his burden could never be offloaded. A survivor's trauma is also part of his legacy. The lives of the murdered cry out against the convenience of oblivion. This is the impulse behind slogans like "Never again!" "Learn from me," he said, in his quiet, humane voice, "learn from me." Read the signs of incitement, racism, incipient violence. Know that words have the habit of becoming deeds, if not immediately, then eventually. This is a baton, the survivor says to his children. And in tacit agreement that such a baton can indeed be handed on, they come to be called the Second Generation. This becomes their burden, whether willingly borne or thrust upon them, but intolerable. Necessary but impossible.

The memory of the period from 1939-1945 was the most vivid of my father's life. He lived that time minute by minute. It pressed to the foreground in his mind. As he aged, other recollections blanched and faded, or were pushed back. These ones remained. It was a doubly cruel blow that survivors lived through the actual events and then were forced to re-live them with increasing vividness in memory towards the end of their lives. The urgency of trauma, like some dreadful cuckoo, supplanted happier memories.

Roman could not sleep for three nights after our visit to Chelmno. Nor could I. He turned in semi-sleep. He got out of bed, paced up and down the small room; no space was large enough for his troubled mind. Watching him in the dark with the night lights of the camp-site palely illuminating his figure, I saw that he could never walk away from what he was carrying within him, nothing could purge his system of the experiences trapped within his cranium. At that hour all spaces, all places were one. That little room was his mind and the world. His agitation was palpable and dreadful. The words he wrote, the memories he painted never rounded nor diluted what he saw.

71

A VISIT TO KARMIEL

On a warm afternoon in July of 2014, I drove up north, through Haifa's Carmel tunnels on the new road, skirting the Kraiot to Acre and then east up into the Western Galilee past the sprawling township of Majd-el-Krum to Karmiel. I parked on one of the older roads, following the upper contours of the hillside with a view north to Lavon and Kfar Vradim, and walked up a thin alley to a small semi-detached house to meet Chanan and Miriam Werbejczyk.

This was the end of the trail that began only a few weeks earlier when Eva Unterman, a lady from Tulsa, Oklahoma, her son Steve, daughter-in-law and three granddaughters visited me. Eva had been a child in the *Metalabteilung*, the metal factory in the Lodz Ghetto run by Alfred Chimowicz. She and her parents were part of the group of 500 slave-labourers sent like my father to Auschwitz, Stutthof and Dresden. She and the other children in that group were the only children ever to leave Auschwitz alive. All others to reach that factory of murder were sent directly to the gas chambers and crematoria.

Eva was not able to answer many of my questions and explained that the things she remembered were different from what an adult remembered but gave me the contact details for two people who might help: Dr Michal Unger and Chanan Werbejczyk. I was moved by Eva's energy and optimism. Her appetite for life reminded me of my father. One of her granddaughters, Phoebe, had illustrated Eva's story in a book both stark and emotive, striking in its directness of Phoebe's identification with her grandmother's experiences. She drew the entire book when she was in her early teens. It is called *Through Eva's Eyes*. Eva's son Steve and I discovered that we were born on the same day, and we were both bemused to note the peculiar cementing effect this had on us.

Two weeks after Eva's family visit, I was sitting on the verandah of Chanan and Miriam Werbejczyk beside a table with lemonade and biscuits and a light breeze stirring the dry heat. The Werbejczyks were clear of mind, bright of eye. They knew that I had questions to ask concerning the escape my father described in his book. Early on Chanan said: "I read your father's book. It is well written but there are inaccuracies, particularly concerning his escape. There are things he did not know or things he did not record."

Miriam listened as Chanan spoke in a quiet, steady voice and occasionally sharpened what he said with a precise detail. Both Chanan and Miriam were from Lodz. Her father, Shmuel Sztajer, bought and sold machines. Avraham Sztajer, her cousin – Avraham who my father had met up with in Netanya, for that short meeting in 2002 – had worked with her father in Lodz. Chanan specialized in lathe-work. Avraham became an expert in the lifting and transfer of machinery, essential to the *Metalabteilung*. The factory had several departments, including a foundry, presses and a forge. It was in one of these departments that the ghetto currency was minted. By mid-1943 the money, gold and other valuables of the Jews of Lodz had been mostly extracted from the Jewish community by the Nazis and most of the Jews had been transported by train to their deaths in Chelmno and Auschwitz. Hans Biebow, the Nazi civilian head of the Lodz Ghetto, and his associates Erich Czarnula and Franz Siefert realised that now that the Jews' goods had been taken, the only remaining asset under their jurisdiction was Jewish labour. And Jewish forced labour was potentially hugely profitable. Now, according to Chanan Werbejczyk and Dr. Michal Unger whom I had met the previous week, the Nazi civilian administrators, fearing that if the ghetto were to be liquidated this would mean the end of their position of comfort and influence. It might also mean them being enlisted and sent to the Russian front, so they focused their energies on creating two factories in the ghetto. One was for prefabricated housing, run by a German construction company from Berlin.

In the words of Dr. Michal Unger:

"More than 600 Jews were allocated to this factory including women and 37 children. They left the ghetto in late October 1944, and eventually most of them reached the concentration camp in Königswusterhausen, a sub camp of Sachsenhausen, near Berlin. Most members of this group were liberated by the Red Army by the end of April 1945.

The second factory was a munitions plant managed also by a private company – Bernsdorf & Co. The group of Jews consisted of 500 people, including entire families. Most worked in the metal factory in the ghetto. This group left the ghetto in late August 1944 and arrived in Auschwitz, where its members remained together without going through selection. To the best of our knowledge, this is the *only* group that arrived in Auschwitz, which did not go through the selection process, and remained intact. Most of the members of this group were transported from Auschwitz to concentration camp Stutthof and in late November 1944 reached Dresden where Biebow and his associates set up a munitions plant known as Bernsdorf & Co. Despite their suffering, mainly in Stutthof, most of its members survived and were liberated in Theresienstadt in May 1945."

These two big factories were connected to the Ministry of Armament, headed by Albert Speer, and were recognized as essential to the war effort.

There was a third group that remained in the ghetto after its liquidation to clean the area and pack up equipment that had been left behind, mainly in the factories. It consisted of approximately

1,000 Jews. This group, like the other two, consisted of workers and Jewish officials. These Jews were liberated by the incoming Soviet forces in January 1945.

Both Miriam's family and Chanan's family worked at the *Metalabteilung,* including his father and mother and his sister and cousins on his and his wife's sides of the family. Metal work was and is in their blood. Today, the manufacturing company Chanan founded is run by his son, but it is Chanan who still designs the newest cutting bits, the router blades and the like, and every day he drives to work at their factory.

Besides perpetuating Biebow, Czarnula and Siefert's roles of authority, all three of the groups in the Lodz Ghetto – the prefabricated housing company, the metal workers, and the ghetto liquidation group meant that the three kingpins had alibis they hoped would help them evade punishment for war crimes.

Dr Michal Unger is clear on this point:

"The paradox is evident: this Nazi war criminal [Hans Biebow], who participated in the annihilation of the Jews of the Lodz ghetto and other ghettos in the Warthegau, rescued a large group of Jews as the war wound down. Even then, he managed to persuade the SS to leave his groups intact. How could he have managed this? Biebow's ability to remove the groups from Auschwitz and Stutthof shows how powerful his connections with the SS must have been."

"But what happened during the escape?" I asked Chanan.

"What makes you think there was just one escape? Many of us escaped. Read my book, I'll give you a copy of *The Black and the Red*. I escaped with four others. We made our way back to Dresden to the factory on Schandauerstrasse. Mr Braun, the works manager who was also a communist, liked us. He later became mayor of one of the boroughs of Dresden. He helped us.

They gave us clothes, cut our hair. They hid us and then we left."

"But were there no SS left? Was it safe to return?"

"Only the SS woman, Gul, was dangerous then. And she was no longer there."

"Were Biebow and Czarnula and Siefert there?"

"Of course," replied Chanan. "They saw us as their passport to safety. They were in the factory the whole time."

"And Sztajer and Szwajcer?" I asked. "How did they escape from the top of the tobacco vats when the others did not? My father to the end of his life must have felt guilty that he could not get the others civilian clothes as he had promised."

"They were never part of that escape with your father. And in his book [the second version] he did not write that they were, said Chanan, clearly and confidently. They were needed to supervise the machines in case the factory needed to be moved from Dresden, west, for the war effort. Then Czarnula sent them out to Oberpoyritz – with Biebow's blessing. The others…"

"Hiding in the tobacco factory…"

"Yes, they were never killed. Said Chanan. None of them was killed, at least not there, not then. Czarnula, Biebow and Braun helped them all. They were all given clothes and a haircut, food, and then they left. There were others besides them and my own group of four who escaped from the march and returned to the factory. I don't know what made Roman think that they died."

"Didn't he ask you about this when he met you?"

"No. I assumed he knew. The only ones to die were those who fell behind on the march to Theresienstadt. Those who were exhausted or ill, they were shot. Most of the others made it."

I stared at my plate. I drank some water and tried to digest what Chanan Werbejczyk has just told me.

My father never asked. He simply had never asked. When they met in 2002, my father never asked Chanan Werbejczyk, the man who knew what had really happened, who could have told him and could have lifted a terrible burden from his mind. I suppose that, for my father, to ask Chanan would have been a partial confession. It was not in his character to do such a thing. Besides, in my father's mind, having made that promise, he always thought that he, he alone, could have saved the others. "We are born alone and we die alone." It was this that caused him to write and rewrite those versions, seeking to find a narrative with which he could live. My father needlessly carried a sense of guilt to the end of his days.

I looked across the garden table from Miriam to Chanan. He sipped his lemonade. There was long pause. I had to ask him once more: "Is it possible that you are mistaken?"

Chanan looked at me and set his hand on the table, face-up. "Ardyn, none of those who escaped was killed, not by Czarnula, Biebow, Siefert or Braun. Not one. They were saving their own skins. They were trying to. They needed as many lives they could get to try and redress the balance. The Russians were coming. It was the end."

72

A SIMPLE BONFIRE

We have a debt to the past but an even greater one to the present and the future, to life and those living now. Consciousness of atrocity – at least for some of the Second Generation – cohabits our minds, like a substratum. The retentive memory, the mind obsessed by the horrors enacted by our species will see alongside or not far way from the cradled infant, the image, the appalling reality of an infant shot or tossed into a furnace. Removed, though not far enough removed from the sexual act will be our knowledge of women raped or mutilated. Sylvia Plath found it impossible to consider the one without being conscious of the other. To her an oven is where bread is baked and also where people were melted and incinerated; lamp shades are made of human skin.

How does one widen our understanding of human hell without also tainting and sullying one's consciousness? Does such knowledge in fact ennoble us? Does awareness of human boundaries make us better social beings, more responsible humans, vigilant to the dangers and pitfalls in the human psyche, alert to the diabolical potential within our species? I want to believe it can. I think it can, but only if we see people as individuals, and, whenever possible, remove symbols and myths from our consciousness. For myths reduce memory while purporting to represent it. Myths have the habit of supplanting history. A people with a history must avoid the creation of slogans, clichés, stock phrases, flags of symbolic convenience – all of which create the outer contour lines that make up myths, whose repetition dulls both ear and tongue.

It took more than a month after our return from Poland for me to start to come up for air. I felt as though I had another journey to make, on my own, to enable me to return to my wife and daughters, even though they were around me and life continued its daily routine. Morning to evening, day after day I worked on the plot of land adjacent our home, clearing scrub weeds, thorny lantana and wild asparagus, cutting low branches, burning them at the day's end, as though enacting some ancient purifying ritual of fire. I worked until I was almost overcome by exhaustion. It took almost the entire month for the flames to become those of a simple bonfire.

NOTES

3. Placing a stone

1. From *Geoffrey Hill and the Tongues Atrocities*, 1978

40. The first death camp

1. My father's second cousin.

47. Duck shoot

1. *Roman's Journey* [Portobello Books, 2007] Amsterdam Publishers, 2023, pp.....

50. The barber's hands

1. In 2009 the German government applied for his extradition from the USA to Germany. He was found guilty, sentenced to life imprisonment and died in prison in 2012.

60. Carrying on

1. We had not visited Stutthof camp on the Baltic Sea. Roman and the film crew decided it was too far to travel to.]

ACKNOWLEDGMENTS

Shlomo Fajner testimony from *Chelmno Witnesses Speak* Konin-Lodz 2004 © The Council for the protection of Memory of combat and martyrdom, the District Museum in Konin. Translated by Jan Lenski, with Shmuel Krakowski.

Roman Halter, *Roman's Journey* [Portobello Books, 2007] Amsterdam Publishers, 2023

Geoffrey Hill, *King Log*, Andre Deutsch, London 1968.

Virginia Woolf, *A Room of One's Own* Speech delivered at Girton College and Newnham College, Cambridge on October 20th and 26th 1928 © The Society of Authors, literary representative of the estate of Virginia Woolf.

Stefan Zweig, *The Post Office Girl*, Sort of Books, London 2008.

With special thanks to Aloma Halter.

And thanks to Gila Shmueli, Stephen Smith, Fergal Keane, Prof. Daniel Reis, Monica Bohm-Duchen, and to Liesbeth Heenk for seeing this through to publication.

ABOUT THE AUTHOR

Ardyn Halter is best known for his painting, printmaking and stained glass.

Born in London, he divides his time between the UK and his home in Israel. Ardyn is the son of Roman Halter whose book *Roman's Journey* has been republished by Amsterdam Publishers.

Ardyn's work is in numerous collections including The British Museum, The Tel Aviv Museum, The Israel Museum, The Victoria and Albert Museum, London, The British Library, London.

He has designed and made the stained glass windows for the National Genocide Memorial in Rwanda, St Johns Wood Synagogue London, Alyth Gardens and Highgate Synagogues, and for Cambridge University.

Previous books include: *The Water's Edge* Lund Humphries,

London 2006; *Out of the Water* Sport, *Diversity and Tolerance, A Portrait of Aqvatikim, Israel's first Masters swimming club English,* Hebrew and Arabic, Israel 2018.

AMSTERDAM PUBLISHERS HOLOCAUST LIBRARY

The series **Holocaust Survivor Memoirs World War II** consists of the following autobiographies of survivors:

Outcry. Holocaust Memoirs, by Manny Steinberg

Hank Brodt Holocaust Memoirs. A Candle and a Promise, by Deborah Donnelly

The Dead Years. Holocaust Memoirs, by Joseph Schupack

Rescued from the Ashes. The Diary of Leokadia Schmidt, Survivor of the Warsaw Ghetto, by Leokadia Schmidt

My Lvov. Holocaust Memoir of a twelve-year-old Girl, by Janina Hescheles

Remembering Ravensbrück. From Holocaust to Healing, by Natalie Hess

Wolf. A Story of Hate, by Zeev Scheinwald with Ella Scheinwald

Save my Children. An Astonishing Tale of Survival and its Unlikely Hero, by Leon Kleiner with Edwin Stepp

Holocaust Memoirs of a Bergen-Belsen Survivor & Classmate of Anne Frank, by Nanette Blitz Konig

Defiant German - Defiant Jew. A Holocaust Memoir from inside the Third Reich, by Walter Leopold with Les Leopold

In a Land of Forest and Darkness. The Holocaust Story of two Jewish Partisans, by Sara Lustigman Omelinski

Holocaust Memories. Annihilation and Survival in Slovakia, by Paul Davidovits

From Auschwitz with Love. The Inspiring Memoir of Two Sisters' Survival, Devotion and Triumph Told by Manci Grunberger Beran & Ruth Grunberger Mermelstein, by Daniel Seymour

Remetz. Resistance Fighter and Survivor of the Warsaw Ghetto, by Jan Yohay Remetz

My March Through Hell. A Young Girl's Terrifying Journey to Survival, by Halina Kleiner with Edwin Stepp

Roman's Journey, by Roman Halter

Memoirs by Elmar Rivosh, Sculptor (1906-1967). Riga Ghetto and Beyond, by Elmar Rivosh

---

The series **Holocaust Survivor True Stories WWII** consists of the following biographies:

Among the Reeds. The true story of how a family survived the Holocaust, by Tammy Bottner

A Holocaust Memoir of Love & Resilience. Mama's Survival from Lithuania to America, by Ettie Zilber

Living among the Dead. My Grandmother's Holocaust Survival Story of Love and Strength, by Adena Bernstein Astrowsky

Heart Songs. A Holocaust Memoir, by Barbara Gilford

Shoes of the Shoah. The Tomorrow of Yesterday, by Dorothy Pierce

Hidden in Berlin. A Holocaust Memoir, by Evelyn Joseph Grossman

Separated Together. The Incredible True WWII Story of Soulmates Stranded an Ocean Apart, by Kenneth P. Price, Ph.D.

The Man Across the River. The incredible story of one man's will to survive the Holocaust, by Zvi Wiesenfeld

If Anyone Calls, Tell Them I Died. A Memoir, by Emanuel (Manu) Rosen

The House on Thrömerstrasse. A Story of Rebirth and Renewal in the Wake of the Holocaust, by Ron Vincent

Dancing with my Father. His hidden past. Her quest for truth. How Nazi Vienna shaped a family's identity, by Jo Sorochinsky

The Story Keeper. Weaving the Threads of Time and Memory - A Memoir, by Fred Feldman

Krisia's Silence. The Girl who was not on Schindler's List, by Ronny Hein

Defying Death on the Danube. A Holocaust Survival Story, by Debbie J. Callahan with Henry Stern

A Doorway to Heroism. A decorated German-Jewish Soldier who became an American Hero, by Rabbi W. Jack Romberg

The Shoemaker's Son. The Life of a Holocaust Resister, by Laura Beth Bakst

The Redhead of Auschwitz. A True Story, by Nechama Birnbaum

Land of Many Bridges. My Father's Story, by Bela Ruth Samuel Tenenholtz

Creating Beauty from the Abyss. The Amazing Story of Sam Herciger, Auschwitz Survivor and Artist, by Lesley Ann Richardson

On Sunny Days We Sang. A Holocaust Story of Survival and Resilience, by Jeannette Grunhaus de Gelman

Painful Joy. A Holocaust Family Memoir, by Max J. Friedman

I Give You My Heart. A True Story of Courage and Survival, by Wendy Holden

In the Time of Madmen, by Mark A. Prelas

Monsters and Miracles. Horror, Heroes and the Holocaust, by Ira Wesley Kitmacher

Flower of Vlora. Growing up Jewish in Communist Albania, by Anna Kohen

Aftermath: Coming of Age on Three Continents. A Memoir, by Annette Libeskind Berkovits

Not a real Enemy. The True Story of a Hungarian Jewish Man's Fight for Freedom, by Robert Wolf

Zaidy's War. Four Armies, Three Continents, Two Brothers. One Man's Impossible Story of Endurance, by Martin Bodek

The Glassmaker's Son. Looking for the World my Father left behind in Nazi Germany, by Peter Kupfer

The Apprentice of Buchenwald. The True Story of the Teenage Boy Who Sabotaged Hitler's War Machine, by Oren Schneider

Good for a Single Journey, by Helen Joyce

Burying the Ghosts, by Sonia Case

American Wolf. From Nazi Refugee to American Spy. A True Story, by Audrey Birnbaum

Bipolar Refugee. A Saga of Survival and Resilience, by Peter Wiesner

The series **Jewish Children in the Holocaust** consists of the following autobiographies of Jewish children hidden during WWII in the Netherlands:

Searching for Home. The Impact of WWII on a Hidden Child, by Joseph Gosler

See You Tonight and Promise to be a Good Boy! War memories, by Salo Muller

Sounds from Silence. Reflections of a Child Holocaust Survivor, Psychiatrist and Teacher, by Robert Krell

Sabine's Odyssey. A Hidden Child and her Dutch Rescuers, by Agnes Schipper

The Journey of a Hidden Child, by Harry Pila and Robin Black

The series **New Jewish Fiction** consists of the following novels, written by Jewish authors. All novels are set in the time during or after the Holocaust.

The Corset Maker. A Novel, by Annette Libeskind Berkovits

Escaping the Whale. The Holocaust is over. But is it ever over for the next generation? by Ruth Rotkowitz

When the Music Stopped. Willy Rosen's Holocaust, by Casey Hayes

Hands of Gold. One Man's Quest to Find the Silver Lining in Misfortune, by Roni Robbins

The Girl Who Counted Numbers. A Novel, by Roslyn Bernstein

There was a garden in Nuremberg. A Novel, by Navina Michal Clemerson

The Butterfly and the Axe, by Omer Bartov

To Live Another Day. A Novel, Elizabeth Rosenberg

A Worthy Life. A Novel, by Dahlia Moore

The series **Holocaust Heritage** consists of the following memoirs by 2G:

The Cello Still Sings. A Generational Story of the Holocaust and of the Transformative Power of Music, by Janet Horvath

The Silk Factory: Finding Threads of My Family's True Holocaust Story, by Michael Hickins

The Fire and the Bonfire. A Journey into Memory, by Ardyn Halter

---

The series **Holocaust Books for Young Adults** consists of the following novels, based on true stories:

The Boy behind the Door. How Salomon Kool Escaped the Nazis. Inspired by a True Story, by David Tabatsky

Running for Shelter. A True Story, by Suzette Sheft

The Precious Few. An Inspirational Saga of Courage based on True Stories, by David Twain with Art Twain

---

The series **WW2 Historical Fiction** consists of the following novels, some of which are based on true stories:

Mendelevski's Box. A Heartwarming and Heartbreaking Jewish Survivor's Story, by Roger Swindells

A Quiet Genocide. The Untold Holocaust of Disabled Children WW2 Germany, by Glenn Bryant

The Knife-Edge Path, by Patrick T. Leahy

Brave Face. The Inspiring WWII Memoir of a Dutch/German Child, by I. Caroline Crocker and Meta A. Evenbly

When We Had Wings. The Gripping Story of an Orphan in Janusz Korczak's Orphanage. A Historical Novel, by Tami Shem-Tov

Jacob's Courage: A Holocaust Love Story, by Charles S. Weinblatt

Want to be an AP book reviewer?

Reviews are very important in a world dominated by the social media and social proof. Please drop us a line if you want to join the *AP review team* and show us at least one review already posted on Amazon for one of our books.
info@amsterdampublishers.com

www.ingramcontent.com/pod-product-compliance
Lightning Source LLC
LaVergne TN
LVHW091547070526
838199LV00024B/575/J